HIDDEN GEMS
of
Italy

AN **INSIDER'S**
SECRET FORMULA
TO **FIND TOP-CLASS**
ITALIAN WINES AT
VALUE PRICES AND
TASTE LA DOLCE VITA

TONY MARGIOTTA

Cover photography and design by Damonza.com

Edited by Melissa Caminneci.

ISBN-13: 978-1976134029

ISBN-10: 1976134021

Library of Congress Control Number

Printed in USA

DOWNLOAD THE AUDIOBOOK FREE!

Just to say thanks for downloading my book, I would like to give you the Audiobook version 100% FREE!

CLICK HERE TO DOWNLOAD

(Or go to gladiatorwine.com/hiddengems-audiobook)

CONTENTS

PART 3: HOW TO SHOP FOR ITALIAN WINES | 107

CHAPTER 1

WHAT THIS BOOK
IS ABOUT

(AND WHAT IT'S NOT ABOUT)

EVEN BEFORE I became an Italian wine importer, I was viewed as a wine expert by my friends. I always had a talent for finding hidden Italian gems at the wine store. What most wine drinkers don't know is that they can do the same thing. Finding a hidden gem just requires some browsing skills.

Do you like to browse?

Don't lie to me now. I know you surf the internet at least two hours a day! So we're just going to filter out the noise, ignore those busy bottles on the shelves, close those nerdy wine apps, forget about those glossy wine magazines, and turn you into a savvy Italian wine shopper that uncovers those hidden gems. In this book, I'm going to teach you how to do two big things:

1. You will learn how to read and understand Italian wine labels.

2. You will learn how to find hidden Italian wine gems (for $20 that taste like $50) at your local wine shop and online.

After you've digested the information in this book you will become an Italian wine guru. You'll be the one who dazzles your friends and family with your amazing wine choices. They will look to you for advice for when they need to buy a wine as a gift.

You'll be the person who makes intelligent purchasing decisions that will please your taste buds while protecting the money in your pocket. While your fellow human beings are chasing the 90-point wines and buying wines based on "the look" of the bottle, you'll be sipping on incredible wines that awaken your senses like never before.

The best part is you don't need to spend a fortune to drink like royalty. This book is a shopping guide for consumers who want to drink luxurious Italian wines at value prices. In this book we will be focusing on quality Italian wines that you can find between $15-$30. For example, I can help you find a $20 bottle that tastes like $50.

From the tips in this book, you'll be drinking in luxury without breaking the bank. These wines are "under-the-radar," top-class, and unknown to mainstream wine enthusiasts. So how do we find these great Italian wines?

I've spent years traveling to Italy, immersing myself into the local wines, studying, tasting and running my wine importing business specializing in hidden gems from Italy. The tips and techniques that I've learned from all my experience have led me to creating a secret shopping formula for wine lovers like you who want to enrich themselves with the hidden gems of Italy. I'm going to share this formula with you and it will become your foundation of knowledge and your method for finding hidden wine gems from Italy.

The truth is that I'm not the only importer who finds hidden gems. There are others. So this secret formula I'm going to share with you is not only the same formula I use when searching for hidden gems in Italy, but it's also the same formula I use when shopping for wine in my hometown of New York City. The tips in this book are for you to use wherever you live and shop for wine, even online shopping.

WHERE MOST AMERICANS GET ITALIAN WINE WRONG

If you've ever traveled to Italy, I bet you had some amazing wines. Then, when you came back home, you felt disappointed with the Italian wine options at your local wine shop. They just weren't on the same level of quality.

You probably wonder why the imported versions of Italian wines don't measure up. You might even blame those damn sulfites. The truth is that it's not the sulfites. Most of the time, when you're drinking Italian wine in America, you're drinking mass-produced, industrially made wines. These are brought to you by what I call "The Big Wine Industry" or BWI.

Maybe you have lucked out and run into some reasonably priced, quality Italian wines on the shelves. But if you play it safe and find yourself drinking the same wines that honestly are not exciting you anymore, you might be experiencing "palate fatigue." It's like eating your favorite food everyday—eventually you have to eat something else because you find yourself not enjoying it as much.

The good news is that you're open-minded enough to realize you need to get something new on your palate. The even better news is that Italy has more variety than you can handle, so there is no reason to ever get bored. With over 2,000 different wine grapes and thousands of wineries in Italy, you certainly can find something to thrill your taste buds.

3 Mistakes That Keep People Away From The Best

According to a survey done on Wine.net in 2015, Americans select wines based on the following:

- —82% of people buy wine based on the price
- —67% of people buy wine based on the brand

This leads us to an interesting conclusion. Most of us buy wines based on our budget and how familiar we are with a brand. 2 out of 3 of us continue to buy "the safe bet," a wine that we're already familiar with. That means all a wine company has to do is outspend their competitors with advertising, price the wine at the sweet spot of $15 and people will buy it like crazy. You could very well be spending your hard-earned money on cheap juice and not even know it!

In the same survey, 24% said they bought the wine based on the label or "the look." At first glance, this seems like a low number, but think about it. That means 1 out of 4 people are buying wine based on whether they like the way the bottle and label look!

These three statistics happen to be the three biggest mistakes people make that are keeping them away from the best Italian wine out there.

I totally understand that price is important to us. We all have to spend within our budget. But when you combine price with selecting only brands you know and a fancy looking bottle, you're going to miss out on some serious hidden gems.

This book will show you there is a much better way to finding top-class Italian wines in the $15-$30 price range.

What This Book is NOT About

This book is NOT about Barolo, Barbaresco, and Brunello di Montalcino, arguably the great wines of Italy. These wines don't fit in the $15-$30 price range and deserve a different discussion for a later book. Yes, the tips in this book will help you find good values for those wines, but a $30 bottle of Barolo is not a hidden gem. In fact, I'd question its authenticity!

This is NOT a guide to help you find a great $10 bottle of wine either. It's economically impossible to find the kinds of quality wines I write about in this book at that price. It's a sad truth.

This book is also NOT a crash course in Italian wines—yet the knowledge you will obtain with this book will lay the foundation to continue learning about Italian wines for the rest of your life. In fact, you will walk away with more knowledge than a typical "Italian Wine for Beginners" would give you. And it can be read in one weekend.

My Life with Wine

I'm Tony Margiotta and I love Italian wines. When I was growing up, I used to go to my Italian grandparents' house on Sundays for dinner. I can remember hot summers sitting at the kitchen table with no air conditioning. Italians are very superstitious about air conditioning; they think it makes you sick. So there used to be a ceiling fan spinning and circulating hot air while my grandmother Margherita was cooking spaghetti, bracciole, meatballs, and broccoli rabe. When we sat down to eat, the fan got turned off.

We sweated our butts off while eating steamy hot spaghetti and a rich red sauce made possible only by Margherita. No one spoke while eating. You just heard silverware tapping the ceramic plates and the "gulp gulp" sound of red wine being poured into my father's and grandfather's glasses.

On special occasions, I was given a shot glass with a little bit of red wine. It made me feel like one of the adults; they'd laugh at me when my face turned a light pink. Those experiences not only took away the taboo of drinking alcoholic beverages as a kid, but they planted the seeds for an appreciation of Italian wine.

Before coming to America, the Margiotta family had a tiny vineyard in the Molise region of Italy. My father's town, Montaquila, is just an hour and half ride by car to Naples. The family made wine just for themselves, plus a little to share with relatives. Decades ago, in the smallest towns of Italian countryside, local people traded their wine for other things that they didn't grow like zucchine or eggplant.

When my father and grandparents left Italy and came to America, they brought their wine culture and implemented it in our family household. It remains intact today.

My grandmother's death in 2000 was a turning point in my life. It was time to go to Italy and connect with my roots. It was always my grandmother's wish that I would go visit her hometown. Even though I was afraid of flying, I went. I continue to go to Italy twice a year.

I fell in love with Italy: the culture, the warm people, the great foods and wine. I went back every summer to visit my relatives. I learned to speak Italian fluently. Most of all, I drank a lot of wine. I would take little trips all over Italy and drink the local wines of the area. It felt like I was living in paradise. I was experiencing what the Italians call "La Dolce Vita," or "The Sweet Life."

From these trips to Italy, I made some very interesting discoveries about Italian wine that I will share with you in this book. These discoveries will bring you closer to authentic, quality Italian wines. Some of these bottles will even challenge your palate, but you'll fall in love with them slowly. And other wines will be love at first sip.

Whenever I got back from my trips to Italy, I'd go to my local wine shops in New York and browse. I began selecting wines that I normally would have overlooked on the shelf. I'd "take a chance," or so it seemed, on a random wine that caught my eye. More and more often I would bring that random wine to a friend's gathering and see that they loved it. My friends and family would compliment my choice, and I suddenly became "the wine expert" of the group. I admit that I was enjoying the reputation.

These savvy wine selections of mine were not by accident. I learned that there were little clues on the front and more clues on the back label of wine bottles that indicated a higher quality. It didn't guarantee that I would like the wine, but it helped me filter out hundreds of wines and narrow my choices down to a select few. The majority of the time, I made wise choices.

Years later, when I started my wine importing company, Gladiator Wine Distribution, I tweaked my formula for selecting wines. It produced even greater results with even more profound wines. I call it the Hidden Gem Formula.

What this book is really about is the real wines of Italy that go unnoticed. These "hidden wines" don't get the attention of the wine magazines or wine shops because they are inundated with "Big Wine Money" from the large industrial producers.

WHAT THIS BOOK WILL TEACH YOU

You're going to learn how to find amazing Italian wines that cost between $15-$30 that are top class! Some of the wines you will find as a result of this book might even be more delicious and cost less than anything you've ever had before.

You're going to learn how to shop for Italian wine at your local wine shop as well as shopping online. I'm going to give you the tips you need to become a savvy wine shopper who can browse the wine shelves and find hidden gems that will surprise your palate and surpass your expectations.

If you're simply a wine lover, and Italian wines seem a little foreign to you, we're going to build a bridge that you can cross easily from what you're drinking now to a new journey into Italian wine, full of surprises and enrichment.

In Part 1 of the book, you'll learn essentials like how to read Italian Wine Labels and the 10 Italian Wine Grapes You Should Know.

You'll learn how to crack the code of the Italian language that you see on wine labels with the Most Important Italian Wine Words To Know included in this book. You'll begin to see word patterns that give clues to what you're drinking, where it's from, and even determine the value of the bottle in your hands.

In Part 2, you'll learn the Hidden Gem Formula and get all my insider tips on what to look for when you're shopping for Italian wine. I'll even destroy the most common myths about Italian wine.

The information in this book will help you filter out the wines unworthy of your money and get you closer to that hidden gem that will enrich not just your palate but the quality of life. You'll be making your own intelligent buying decisions without depending on critic's scores and "the look" of the label.

When you implement the Hidden Gem Formula and other tips in this book, you will enable yourself to make in-the-know buying decisions so that you can drink in luxury, excite your palate, and share luscious wines that will make your friends and family so happy. You will be living "La Dolce Vita." Are you ready to taste it?

CHAPTER 2

LIQUID TRAVEL: THE WINE TASTING EXPERIENCE

WELCOME TO MY kitchen table. It's the place where I drink my favorite Italian wines, share stories with family and friends, and pause frequently to swirl, sniff, and sip.

The juice in my glass traveled over 4,000 miles from an Italian vineyard to my table in Manhattan. The grapes that were squashed to make that juice traveled even further. Not by distance, but through history; some 2500 years back. This evening I'm drinking one of my favorite wines, a Perricone from the Castellucci Miano winery in Sicily. Perricone is Sicily's oldest existing red grape – over 2500 years old.

I like using the traditional corkscrew to pop the cork. Those new bottle-open gadgets drive me crazy sometimes; they don't even look like corkscrews anymore! They have more arms than an octopus. So I take my old-school corkscrew and pop the cork.

While I pour the soul-serving elixir into a large wine glass, the pouring taps the glass gently like the sound of a stream in the forest.

The wine gradually flows like a river until the most powerful sounds of red liquid slosh against the half-filled glass, climaxing like a waterfall.

I always keep my wine under an imagined halfway mark in the glass because I'm obsessed with leaving enough space to swirl and smell. Before I swirl, I'll take a look deep into the wine in my glass on a 45-degree angle so I can see the different shades of red and purple. Transparent ruby red on the outer rims of the liquid act as trampolines while micro lights sporadically bounce off the wine like a shower of shooting stars. Now it's time to move in closer with my nose to smell my drink's mysterious and pleasing aromas. I find that the great wines of the Old World tend to have more mysterious aromas than the New World California wines. It forces my nose to go back and attempt to solve the mystery every time I take another sip.

As I begin to sip from my chalice, I feel like I'm about to enter a portal that takes me to the ancient lands where the Perricone grapes' origins bore fruit. When I'm drinking Perricone, I'm not in my kitchen. I'm in the Madonie Mountains of Sicily, the same place the ancient Romans explored to enjoy the grapes of the gods. *High mountain tops, berry bushes, slopes of trees and no civilization in sight.* I feel connected to the Sicilian earth.

As my liquid vacation continues, mature dark fruits coalesce with my lips and as the wine flows to the middle of my palate; ripe raspberries prickle and add brightness like the sun rising on the eastern slopes; a spicy blend of black pepper, chili, and cinnamon slice softly on the swallow; and the finish leaves soft tannins like wings gliding over puffy clouds. The landing opens those clouds filled with oozing forest berries and then volcanic earth tones touchdown on my molars.

Whenever friends invite me to their home for dinner I bring this wine quite often. No one has ever heard of it. When they do taste it, there is a sudden moment of silence while they process these new flavors, aromas, and texture that trail-blazes a new path through their palates. Then the compliments flow. "Tony this is a great wine! Thank you so much for bringing this! How on Earth did you find it?!" Everyone is looking at me and smiling. I made my friends happy. It's a rewarding feeling.

CHAPTER 3

WHAT KINDS OF ITALIAN WINES ARE OUT THERE?

IT'S MY OPINION that Italian wines are the best in the world. There is no country on Earth with the range of biodiversity in the soils, micro climates, and the largest selection of native grape varietals than Italy.

The best part about Italian wine is that you can never get bored because Italy has about 2,000 native grape varietals used for wine-making. That means thousands of wines, endless flavors, and limitless experiences for you! Boredom is impossible.

It might be easier to buy a California Cabernet or a trendy Sauvignon Blanc from New Zealand, but most wine lovers have a deep respect for Italian wines. It's just that Italian wines seem to be so much more difficult to understand when you don't know what to buy and you don't know where to start.

Most wine drinkers know two categories of Italian wine:

1. The $10 cheap wines: the straw-covered Chianti, the bubbly Prosecco, and the "safe bet" Pinot Grigio.

2. The expensive and world renowned Italian wines: Barolo, Barbaresco, and Brunello.

On the low end, you've got the cheap Italian wines that don't really show you the world-class potential of the "land of wine." On the high end, you've got some of the best wines in the world, from $40 and up. Even on the high end though, it's not guaranteed that every Barolo, Barbaresco, or Brunello will be any good. The high-end wines require different hidden gem seeking skills – but that's for another book.

Here's the deal: you can actually find high quality, top-class, hidden gem Italian wines in the $15-$30 price range. This is a third, unexplored category that we will focus on in this book.

Anyone who has ever traveled the country extensively will tell you that every region in Italy has a different cuisine. There are virtually thousands of different pasta dishes in Italy that all taste different. You'll never get bored with the same tired dishes; Italy always has something new to offer your palate! The same holds true with wine. The best part is we have access to virtually all the wines of Italy's 20 regions. Especially the $15-$30 range I'm talking about.

That's a lot of wine choices to deal with. I'll go another step further. Besides all the different grape varietals and regions, there are many types of Italian wines that you should avoid. But it is easy to avoid these wines when you know what to look for; there are clues on the front and back labels of a bottle of wine that reveal the quality and value of that wine. These clues on a bottle will help you decide whether to buy it and try it, or let it collect dust on the store shelf.

The wine world is big business. Everyone wants to get into the game and make a profit. If you ever heard in the news that there is a worldwide wine shortage, I can tell you that that is one of the biggest lies I know of in the wine business. This is a ploy by the Big Wine Industry to get people to buy more and spend more money on wine. Don't fall for it. Wine is Italy's #1 exported product and the country always produces more than it can export.

I don't know about you, but I don't want to drink the same thing all the time. In the summer, I want to be sipping on a refreshing Catarratto from Sicily or pairing a massive Aglianico from Campania with my Ribeye Steak. I want to hang out with my friends on a summer evening drinking a bubbly Falanghina Spumante or sharing a Montepulciano d'Abruzzo with my family at a Sunday dinner.

So there are many motivations behind selecting an Italian wine. But the one thing that we can be sure of is that we are seeking hidden gems that take our palate to paradise while protecting our pockets.

CHAPTER 4

WHAT IS THE HIDDEN GEM FORMULA?

IMAGINE YOURSELF WALKING into a wine shop. The shelves are full of dark glass bottles. The floors are covered in cardboard boxes filled with grape juice. You're surrounded by thousands of bottles that all want your attention.

Maybe there's someone at the store who approaches you and offers help. Maybe no one comes to help you at all. Maybe you're a little hesitant to ask for a recommendation.

A wine shop can be intimidating at times. Some of us don't want to look like we don't know what we're doing!

Enter the Hidden Gem Formula

I developed the Hidden Gem Formula for my importing business to uncover hidden wine gems from Italy. In this book, I'm going to share with you the keys that I use to find hidden gems so that you can do the same no matter where you live in the world.

You'll use this secret formula to help you shop savvy at your local wine shops and even online. The techniques I use on the wine trails in Italy will be the same techniques you will use to help you filter out the noise and uncover those hidden gems.

In this guide, I've also included a "Ferrari Fast Cheat Sheet" if you feel like just skipping over some of the finer points and getting to the quick tips now. When you have the time, read the book from cover to cover so you can dig in deeper and unearth the secrets to Italian wine. Learning about Italian wines should ultimately become a lifelong hobby of yours, and this book is just the beginning.

PART 1

CRACKING THE CODE:

HOW TO READ ITALIAN
WINE LABELS

CHAPTER 5

HOW TO READ ITALIAN WINE LABELS

B EFORE WE EVEN think about shopping for Italian wine, we need to demystify Italian wine labels both front and back.

In this chapter, we are going to break down the keys of the front and back labels. Think of these keys as "clues" to what type of wine you're holding in your hands. You'll also begin to see patterns repeatedly once you know what to look for.

Take a look at the graphic below, the Italian Wine Pyramid. This is how I want you to be thinking about Italian wines, from top to bottom. Notice how this upside down pyramid narrows until we get to the producer's name. You're going from something big and wide like the whole country of Italy, to something smaller like a region, to something even more targeted like a sub-region inside a region, then targeting a single grape in that region and finally, the producer who makes the wine. The producer is the most important aspect to finding a hidden gem. The producer is more important than any vintage chart or review. You'll find out why in Part 2.

Italian Pyramid

How To Think
About Italian Wines

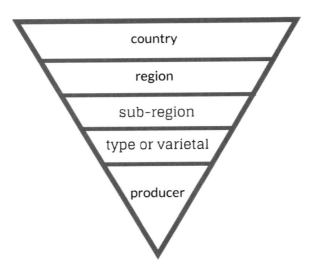

country

region

sub-region

type or varietal

producer

In the infographic example below, you'll see that I filled in the information for the pyramid. The country we're looking at is Italy—that's the easy part! Then we've got to figure out which of the 20 regions in Italy that the wine comes from. In this case it's Sicily. Next is the sub-region which is Sicilia DOC. Notice how I attached the DOC after the sub-region. More on that later. The grape that the wine is made of is called Catarratto and the producer's name is Castellucci Miano.

Italian Pyramid

How To Think
About Italian Wines

| Italy |
| Sicily |
| Sicilia DOC |
| Catarratto |
| Castellucci Miano |

Essentially, Italian wines are to be understood in terms of geography, grape, and the producer. When I'm drinking Italian wine, I'm always thinking about the region and sub-region it comes from, the grape it's made with, and the producer's name. Most of the front label of a wine bottle will have this info. So you should look out for these elements. Over time, they will give you a sense as to what the wine will taste like even if you've never had it before.

But here's the one thing that can make Italian wines confusing. Besides the keys in the Italian Wine Pyramid, you might see some words that indicate a wine type, a nickname, or the name of the town that it comes from. In the next few chapters, we'll go over all of this with examples and break it down layer by layer.

CHAPTER 6

REGIONS

I TALY IS MADE up of 20 regions, kind of like 20 states. Each region has its own native grapes that produce distinct wines. I've included a map of these regions below.

To learn how to pronounce Italy's regions, you can go to my YouTube channel and watch me pronounce them: https://www.youtube.com/channel/UCX2azuteOuIvU3z2rLi3PAw

Here's a map of Italy's 20 regions below:

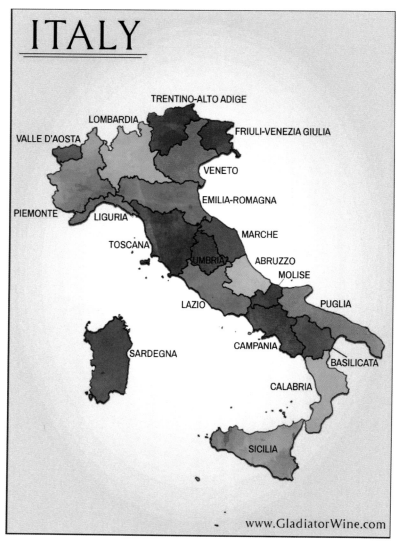

So what do we do with them?

Look at the Italian Wine Pyramid to see how you should be organizing Italian wines in your mind so you can remember what you like, what you don't like, where it's from, what's it made of, and who made it.

This will help you organize your mind as you begin to learn about the different grape varietals in Italy and which region they're grown in. It sounds like a lot of work, but it's a life long journey. I promise you'll never get bored and your taste buds will thank you for it!

CHAPTER 7

CLASSIFICATIONS

Have you ever seen the three letters DOC on Italian wine labels? It can also be spelled out: Denominazione di Origine Controllata

The Italian government and Italian wineries have invested tons of money into ensuring that their products meet certain quality standards. This is both an effort to ensure authenticity as to how the wine was made and to assure consumers that the product is of quality. Below are 5 different government classifications of Italian wines that you'll see on the front and/or back wine labels coming from Italy.

1. DOCG - Denominazione di Origine Controllata e Garantita

2. DOC - Denominazione di Origine Controllata

3. IGT - Indicazione Geographica Tipica

4. DOP - Denominazione di Origine Protetta

5. IGP - Indicazione Geographica Protetta

The first 3 classifications are strictly used for Italian wines. The

DOCG is considered to be a wine that has met the strictest guidelines by the Italian government for how the wine was made and where it can be made. The DOCG usually indicates a "sub-region" or "appellation" which is a very precise, small area where the wine can be produced and where the grapes can grow. There are several lab tests and analyses to pass to obtain this classification. DOCG is considered to be the highest quality wine because of its stringent regulations.

The DOC classification has less strict rules compared to the DOCG but very important for quality standards. A DOC zone can be designated to a region, sub-region or appellation. For example, in the Abruzzo region, you might see a Montepulciano d'Abruzzo DOC, which is a high quality Montepulciano wine that can come from almost anywhere in the whole region. Why? Because Montepulciano d'Abruzzo means "Montepulciano grapes from Abruzzo." Since Abruzzo is a region, and has a DOC classification, it means that virtually any area in the Abruzzo region that grows Montepulciano grapes can obtain the DOC so long as they follow the quality regulations. Notice on the map below that I circled the whole region of Abruzzo and that number 5 is one of the DOC classifications that in fact, covers the whole region.

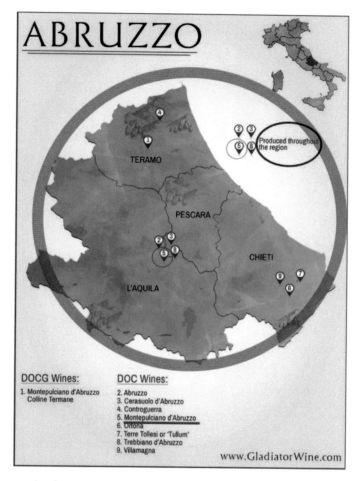

Instead of a DOC zone that covers a whole region, you're more likely to see a DOC designated to a much smaller area of land, which for now, we'll call it a sub-region. We'll cover sub-regions in more detail in the next chapter.

Let's look at another DOC example. Look for #6 in the graphic below. You'll see that Eloro DOC indicates Eloro as the sub-region. I've attached a DOC wine map of Sicily so you can see what I'm talking about. In the Sicily map, you'll see circled the tiny area called

Eloro which is number 6. Eloro happens to be one of the DOC sub-regions for Sicily's most produced red grape: Nero d'Avola.

In this case, you will see on the front label of a bottle of wine, Nero d'Avola, the grape name, and Eloro DOC directly below it on the front label to indicate the sub-region and classification.

If you've tasted a wine from this area in Sicily before, it will give you a sense as to what it tastes like if you ever find a different producer from that area.

The classifications are always tied to the sub-region where the grapes are grown and where the wine is made. From the two examples before, you learned that a classification could be tied to an entire region or a sub-region. But they are usually tied to sub-regions most of the time. Understanding Italian wines requires some geography skills. Think of it like a treasure map!

Let's look at one more example on the Sicily map below. There is only one DOCG in Sicily, called Cerasuolo di Vittoria. You'll see it as number 1 on the map. The difference between the Cerasuolo di Vittoria DOCG and the other DOC sub-regions is that higher quality standards are required to achieve that classification. How is this all figured out? The Italian government decides.

The third classification on the list, the IGT classification, came into being in the 70's when producers in Tuscany made a red blend called "Super Tuscan." The wine had French grapes like Cabernet and Merlot blended with their local Sangiovese grapes. The Super

Tuscan producers couldn't get a DOC classification because they were blending Italian grapes with French grapes, so they lobbied to create this classification. Since then, the IGT has evolved into larger geographical areas within regions, so that producers whose vineyards are located outside of the DOC/DOCG sub-regions can obtain a classification of quality from the Italian government. The requirements are less stringent than a DOC, and the beauty is that producers have more freedom to create excellent wines using techniques outside of the DOC/DOCG restrictions.

The last two additions of Italian classification are:

1. DOP - Denominazione di Origine Protetta

2. IGP - Indicazione Geographica Protetta

Welcome to some major confusion! These two were invented by the European Union and they are used to classify both food products and wine! Thanks EU for creating more confusion!

The DOP classification is on par with both the DOC and the DOCG classifications according to the EU. In actuality, the DOP is on the same level as the DOC. The DOCG still remains the supreme leader in quality standards. That doesn't mean you should avoid wines without DOCG. Quite the contrary as you'll discover throughout this book.

The last one, IGP, is the same thing as IGT. There is no difference worth discussing. The IGT/IGP label is used for several reasons:

1. The winery's vineyards are located outside of the boarders of the DOC/DOCG zones.

2. The winery chooses to have greater flexibility as to how they make their wines.

3. The grape varietal used in the wine might be made in such small quantities that the government has not yet classified or will not classify the grape as a DOC or DOCG.

The best way to understand classifications is to look at Italian wine maps like the ones included in this book. But there are so many more. Sign up to the Hidden Gems Club and I'll let you know when my webinar is released so you can see visually how to figure this all out with me as your guide. The deeper you're willing to go into the world of Italian wine, the more your palate will be rewarded!

INSIDER THOUGHTS

From my experience, a DOCG classification doesn't guarantee that the wine will taste good. It does guarantee that the wine was made with the strictest standards to accurately express the sub-region of origin that the wine comes from. However, there are many wineries that make world class wines that are located outside of the DOCG territories. For me, the classifications don't matter all that much as long as you follow the Hidden Gem Formula.

Another issue I have with the coveted DOC's and DOCG's is that there are many rare grape varietals in Italy that haven't been made in large-enough quantities to get the Italian government to assign them a DOC zone. And yet, there are artisans who practice the strictest standards in the vineyard and cellar to cultivate these rare grapes and make world class wines with them. They will only receive the IGT or IGP classification. We just need to figure which IGT's are high quality. I know how to do that, and you will too as long as you follow the Hidden Gem Formula in Part 2.

It's been my experience that if you find a wine that is outside the DOC and DOCG sub-regions on the map, then the winery is forced to use the IGT classification even if they practice even stricter standards than those with the DOC and DOCG classifications. As with everything in Italy, there are exceptions. The main point here is that I don't want you making your purchasing decisions based on the classification alone. It's not a shortcut that I want you using because you'll miss out on some extraordinary wine.

Take a look at the region of Abruzzo. They make one of the most popular Italian wines, the Montepulciano d'Abruzzo. You can see on the Abruzzo wine map that it doesn't really matter where the vineyards are located in the region; as long as the winery passes the guidelines, they can get the Montepulciano d'Abruzzo DOC classification.

Some wineries make 100% Montepulciano wines that fall under the IGT guidelines because the winemaker has more freedom to experiment in the wine cellar. The wines can be very good and distinctly express a micro territory in Italy.

In other wine regions, the winery's vineyards might be located a few kilometers outside of the DOC zone. If there is no "regional DOC" like Montepulciano d'Abruzzo, then the winery can't get the classification. That doesn't make them bad. The borders were chosen by the government, and they can be a bit arbitrary. Searching for high quality IGT wines is one of several keys in the Hidden Gem Formula, and we'll dig deeper into it in Part 2.

Regardless, I want you to look for these classifications on the front and back labels. It's important to know because if a producer makes an amazing wine that is also a DOCG, it will probably command a higher price at your wine shop. This is how the price of a wine can be justified.

Another example to illustrate classification importance is Prosecco, the Italian sparkling white wine. Authentic Prosecco must come from the Veneto region, and it will contain either a DOC or DOCG classification.

In the news recently, we heard about wineries in Germany and other Italian regions producing Prosecco. They were putting the word "Prosecco" on the bottle, but technically, authentic Prosecco can only come from Veneto. You won't see a DOC or DOCG on those bottles. That's why it's important to learn about Italian grapes and which regions they originate from. You don't want to be duped into buying a wine that is not authentic.

If the wine you're looking at does not show any classification—don't buy it! It means that the wine is considered Table Wine or *Vino da Tavola*. Honestly it's not worth the money because it's the lowest quality wine exported from Italy. It usually tastes like rusted iron if you ask me.

CHAPTER 8

SUB-REGIONS

THE VARIETY OF Italian wine is so vast that just indicating a region name like Tuscany or Sicily on the bottle isn't enough to specify where it's from and what it might taste like. It's kind of like comparing the wines of Napa Valley in California to wines in Sonoma. Both wines come from the same state, but within that state are different wine zones. Italian regions have a thousand times more variety.

To allow more specificity as to the origin of an Italian wine, the Italians came up with "sub-regions." Sub-regions are wine zones that make special local wines that express the unique land, soil, and climate of that tiny area. In the wine world, the word "appellation" is used but for now let's use "sub-region" because it clearly means "an area within a region."

Once you've memorized the 20 regions of Italy, you can begin spending more time getting to know a single region by exploring the sub-regions within it.

For example, let's take a look at a red wine grape called Primitivo.

It grows in the Puglia region. When you look at the Puglia wine map below, you will see a few dozen sub-regions tied to DOC classifications. Primitivo grows in most of those sub-regions. Depending on where it grows, it will taste very different. It will share some characteristics since it's the same grape, but if you were to open up three bottles from different sub-regions, you'd clearly notice a difference.

PUGLIA

⑤ Produced throughout the region

BARLETTA-ANDRIA-TRANI
FOGGIA
BARI
TARANTO
BRINDISI
LECCE

DOCG Wines:
1. Castel del Monte Bombino Nero
2. Castel del Monte Nero di Troia Riserva
3. Castel del Monte Rosso Riserva
4. Primitivo di Manduria Dolce Naturale

DOC Wines:
5. Aleatico di Puglia
6. Alezio
7. Barletta
8. Brindisi
9. Cacc'e mmitte di Lucera
10. Castel del Monte
11. Colline Joniche Taratine
12. Copertino
13. Galatina
14. Gioia del Colle
15. Gravina
16. Leverano
17. Lizzano
18. Locorotondo
19. Martina
20. Matino
21. Moscato di Trani
22. Nardo
23. Negroamaro di Terra d'Otranto
24. Orta Nova
25. Ostuni
26. Primitivo di Manduria
27. Rosso di Cerignola
28. Salice Salentino
29. San Severo
30. Squinzano
31. Tavogliere delle Puglie
32. Terra d'Otranto

www.GladiatorWine.com

If you're new to Italian wines, you should be aware that some of the words on the wine label will indicate a sub-region. Pay attention to the sub-regions because this could be a clue for you that you have found a hidden gem that pleases your taste buds!

What does this all mean for you?

Let's say you want to explore the wines of Puglia. Just by looking at the wine map, you have 32 different wine recommendations! Now there are hundreds of producers in Puglia that make these different types of wine. But you could pick just two each weekend that cost between $15-$25 a bottle. You could also get together with your friends and family and do a "Puglia Night." Each person would bring a wine from the wine map, cover up the bottles so you can't see which one you're tasting, and vote on your favorite one. Whichever wine wins would beg this question: Did the wine win because of the sub-region it comes from or because of the producer that makes it? Your next "wine night" would be a "sub-region" night where you bring a wine only from that sub-region but made by different producers. Play the same game and see what you discover.

My favorite Primitivo comes from Salento, a sub-region of Puglia. Notice how there is no Salento in the Puglia wine map above. Why? This leads us to the IGT classifications. Salento is classified only as an IGT in Puglia. If you look at the wine maps I gave you so far, there are only DOC and DOCG sub-regions listed on the map. If I included the IGT's on the same wine map, it would be a mess to look at. Let me show you an example below.

PUGLIA

⑤ Produced throughout the region

BARLETTA-ANDRIA-TRANI

FOGGIA

BARI

Salento

TARANTO

BRINDISI

LECCE

DOCG Wines:
1. Castel del Monte Bombino Nero
2. Castel del Monte Nero di Troia Riserva
3. Castel del Monte Rosso Riserva
4. Primitivo di Manduria Dolce Naturale

DOC Wines:
5. Aleatico di Puglia
6. Alezio
7. Barletta
8. Brindisi
9. Cacc'e mmitte di Lucera
10. Castel del Monte
11. Colline Joniche Taratine
12. Copertino
13. Galatina
14. Gioia del Colle
15. Gravina
16. Leverano
17. Lizzano
18. Locorotondo
19. Martina
20. Matino
21. Moscato di Trani
22. Nardo
23. Negroamaro di Terra d'Otranto
24. Orta Nova
25. Ostuni
26. Primitivo di Manduria
27. Rosso di Cerignola
28. Salice Salentino
29. San Severo
30. Squinzano
31. Tavogliere delle Puglie
32. Terra d'Otranto

www.GladiatorWine.com

Notice how Salento covers a larger area than the tiny DOC zones. That means any wines that are made outside of the DOC zones or wines made that didn't follow the DOC rules, would be classified as Salento IGT wines in that area of Puglia.

What's the difference between a sub-region and an appellation?

When we're dealing with Italian wines, there are two types of sub-regions: geographical areas and appellations. They are both tied to the classifications. A geographical sub-region will be marked with IGT or IGP, indicating a larger geographical area within a region. Taking from the example on the Puglia map from before, Salento IGT indicates a large geographical area called Salento which is found in the southern section of the Puglia region.

An appellation sub-region will be marked with either DOC, DOP or DOCG, which usually indicates a much smaller piece of territory. Example: Primitivo di Manduria which is number 26 on the Puglia map. Occasionally, a DOC can cover an entire region if the grape used is super important to that region. For example, Montepulciano d'Abruzzo can be classified as a DOC anywhere in the Abruzzo region. But it's not typical. Usually DOC and DOCG are tiny little areas inside a region.

Understanding the classifications and sub-regions are probably the most difficult parts of this book, but they are essential if you want to be able to read Italian wine labels. You won't be able to find a hidden gem without the ability of reading labels. At the end of Part 1, I'm going to give you a list of action steps to do that will help you recognize instantly the parts of a wine label. Once you've done that, you'll begin to look for these things on Italian wine labels both front and back. After a while you'll begin to see the same patterns over and over again. Even without learning the Italian language you'll know what you're looking at simply by pattern recognition.

CHAPTER 9

ITALIAN TOWNS AND NICKNAMES

Is Sangiovese a grape or a wine? **It's both.** Is Chianti a grape or a wine? **It's a wine.** Therein lies an annoying problem with Italian wines.

Sometimes Italian wines tell you the name of the grape by putting it on the front label, and sometimes they'll put a name of a town on it instead. Sometimes they get even more creative and give the bottle a nickname.

An example of a "town wine" would be Chianti. You'll never see the grape name, Sangiovese, on the front of a Chianti bottle. Chianti is a type of Italian wine that is named after the town it comes from, Chianti. The interaction of the Sangiovese grape, the soil, and the climate of Chianti all interact in a way that makes it a distinct wine with a unique flavor profile and character.

Another example is Barolo, which is the name of a town in the Piemonte region. Barolo is made with the Nebbiolo grape. Its distinct flavors and textures are only possible because of precisely where the wine is made.

Naming a bottle of wine after a specific town is more common in the Northern regions of Italy than the Southern ones. Here's one from Southern Italy: Taurasi. This wine comes from a town called Taurasi in the Campania region, and it's made with Aglianico grapes. In the next chapter, you'll see an infographic with the most popular Italian wines named after a town.

Finally, to make things even more complicated, Italian wineries sometimes give their bottles nicknames. Here's a picture of a Castellucci Miano "Miano" Sicilia IGT 2011. When you look at the classification, you'll see it says "Sicilia IGT" which is the classification and sub-region. In this case Sicilia IGT is referring to the whole region of Sicily. They also have in cursive the name, "Miano." This bottle was given a short nickname after the winery. How do I know that? Do the actions steps at the end of Part 1 and you'll easily be able to figure it out.

nickname

Sometimes winery owners will even name a wine after their spouse or after their grandfather. It will be easier to spot these after looking at dozens of wine labels. You'll start to see common patterns reappearing.

Later in the book, I'll also give you some of the most common Italian words that you'll see on wine labels.

In the end, there is no way of you knowing, just by looking at a bottle of Italian wine, as to which words are a grape varietal, a town, or a nickname. But you must learn them so that you can get access to the hidden gems of Italy. At the end of part 1, I'll make it easier for you. You'll get a list of action steps to memorize and then you'll apply that information by looking at wine labels to see if you can decode them.

CHAPTER 10

SIX WINES NAMED AFTER ITALIAN TOWNS

Chianti
Region: Toscana
Grape: 80-100% Sangiovese
Dry Red

Barolo
Region: Piemonte
Grapes: Nebbiolo
Dry Red

Barbaresco
Region: Piemonte
Grapes: Nebbiolo
Dry Red

Taurasi

Region: Campania
Grape: Aglianico
Dry Red

Soave
Region: Veneto
Grape: Garganega 70 - 100%
Dry White

Bardolino
Region: Veneto
Grapes: Corvinone, Molinara, Rondinella
Dry Red

CHAPTER 11

THE MAP TECHNIQUE

THE TECHNIQUE I'M about to show you cannot be found in any of the professional wine literature but it has played a key role in my ability to find amazingly delicious Italian wines. Through my years of traveling in Italy, I spent a lot of time looking at maps.

When I began traveling the country, there was no GPS, and no Google Maps. There were only these large, fold-out type of maps that you could buy at bookstores and gas stations. Then years later we evolved into using maps on our smart phones.

My love for maps goes all the way back to my childhood. My mother bought a puzzle for me that she thought would be both fun and educational. It was made of hundreds of little pieces that took many hours to put together. When I finally put all the pieces together, it showed the map of the United States. Then I'd take the puzzle apart, flip over the pieces, and put them together again. On the other side of the puzzle was a map of the whole world. I would spend hours and hours putting together and taking apart this puzzle.

I was fascinated with the colors, the shapes, and the names of the states, capital cities, and countries.

Without my mom's educational gift, I might never have developed a love for geography. It would take many years more, but I began to apply my passion for geography into seeking out hidden wine gems by using the map of Italy.

Through trial and error of tastings, I began to notice that certain regional wines shared common qualities and that those qualities could be tied to the province that they come from. For example, Montepulciano d'Abruzzo wines made in the Province of Pescara, (PE) had more tart fruit notes and acidity on the front palate compared to the round and mature ripe fruit notes in the Montepulciano d'Abruzzo wines from the Province of Chieti, (CH).

Once you get comfortable with reading Italian wine labels I highly suggest you experiment with the information in this chapter.

Every time you have a bottle of Italian wine, I want you to turn it around and look at the back label. You are going to comb through all the words like a detective using a magnifying glass to solve a puzzle. You will be looking for two letters in parenthesis. Not all labels have these two letters, but when they do, it will give you a clue as to the quality and character of the wine in your hand. But the quality of that wine is ultimately up to you and your taste.

The first time you do this, you will get zero results. This is a technique that will benefit you over time as you look for the province for every bottle of wine you drink. With each new bottle, you will make note of the province and you will eventually begin to see common characteristics between producers from the same province. You will also notice the same wine types from different provinces will result in wines of a different character.

The two letters in parenthesis represent the name of a province. Regions are like states, and provinces are like capital cities. All the little towns or villages surrounding a particular area will fall under the control of one of these provinces. Often times, a winery will write on the back label the name of the town where they are located followed by the province name, usually in parenthesis.

Valle d'Aosta is a region with one province because it's so small, but Sicily has nine provinces because it's a huge region. Therefore, it's less important to learn the province of Valle d'Aosta while it's very important to distinguish between the provinces of Sicily.

WHY IS THE PROVINCE IMPORTANT?

Well, you might discover that you like Cannonau wines that come from the province of Nuoro (NU). You might like Primitivo di Manduria from the Province of Taranto, (TA). This code can give you a general idea of where the vineyards are located and what they might taste like.

You might equally discover that you don't like Nero d'Avola wines that come from (TP), the province of Trapani, but you like Nero d'Avola from the Province of Palermo (PA). This a fascinating technique to help you filter down the limitless choices on the shelf to the wines that come from the provinces that please your palate.

Below you will see a provincial map of Italy for your reference. You can also download a free printable version or a JPEG file so you can zoom in closer to see the provinces. Click on the link or copy/paste the link below for the map and other free bonuses.

http://gladiatorwine.com/hiddengems/

Among other bonuses, I created a spread sheet of all the provinces in Italy with their two-letter codes. I broke down all the provinces by region so you can find them more easily. Download it free here: http://gladiatorwine.com/hiddengems/

As you dive deeper into Italian wines, use the map technique while you sip on your next Cannonau and begin your treasure hunt for gems that please your palate.

CHAPTER 12

10 ITALIAN WINE GRAPES YOU SHOULD KNOW

W HILE CABERNET SAUVIGNON and Chardonnay are both grapes used for winemaking, they are not Italian grapes of origin. They originate from France which makes them native French grapes. These two grapes have evolved commercially into "international varietals" because they are grown in wine regions all over the world. Depending on where these grapes are grown, you'll experience a wine that tastes very different from one place to another.

I personally can't stand international varietals for this reason. The corporatization of wine by the Big Wine Industry is taking the passion and soul of wine away from us. The industrialization of wine has become kind of like the soda industry; a beverage that is easily replicable and controllable for taste and marketability. There are places in the world that simply shouldn't be making wine, but modern techniques in the vineyard and in the cellar allow them to do so. But I digress.

Italy is the home of about 2,000 native grape varietals. You'll never know them all, but it will be fun trying! I'm going to help you turn your passion for Italian wines into a lifelong hobby by giving you the first 10 Italian grape varietals that you should explore.

These Top 10 grape varietals are based on national production levels, not my top ten favorites. They are the top 10 most produced grape varietals of native origin in Italy. Each of these work well as single varietal wines so you can experience the essence of a single grape in your glass. For this reason, I omitted only one grape from this list, Trebbiano Toscano, because it's a blending grape.

After you feel like you know these varietals, I recommend that your next step be to explore other grape varietals by region. Sign up for a free account to Hidden Gems and I'll send you for free the most important grapes of each region.

TOP TEN MOST PRODUCED ITALIAN GRAPE VARIETALS

1. Sangiovese (red) (Tuscany / all over Italy)

2. Montepulciano (red or rosé) (Abruzzo / Molise)

3. Catarratto (white) (Sicily)

4. Barbera (red) (Piemonte)

5. Nero d'Avola (red) (Sicily)

6. Primitivo (red) (Puglia)

7. Moscato (sweet white) (Piemonte / all over Italy)

8. Negroamaro (red or rosé) (Puglia)

9. Garganega (white) (Veneto)

10. Trebbiano (white) (Abruzzo)

WHAT DO THEY TASTE LIKE?

Sangiovese: This is the most produced red grape varietal in Italy. The grape is found in world famous wines like Chianti and Brunello di Montalcino. The grape tastes different depending on where the grapes are grown and who makes the wine. You'll find both medium-bodied Sangiovese and massive full-bodied ones.

A good Sangiovese tastes like lightly sour red cherries that make your eyes pop with excitement. The taste quickly changes to dark red cherries that savor your senses, and it leaves a melted cocoa powder aspect on the finish when oaked. Even though Tuscany is the most known region for Sangiovese, I'd recommend trying the varietal from other regions as well. Sangiovese is an age-worthy grape, but the producer is key to finding an age-worthy version.

Montepulciano: The second most produced grape in Italy is Montepulciano, a red grape. The most famous Montepulciano wines come from the Abruzzo region. Abruzzo is where you'll also find one of the best types of rosé in Italy, Cerasuolo d'Abruzzo. The rosé versions are deep and complex. They have more body than most rosé: they are much drier than the sugar-bomb blushes and more complex than those trendy pink rosés that look like Vitamin Water. Cerasuolo d'Abruzzo rosé usually feature bright red fruit and dried candy notes.

Montepulciano d'Abruzzo makes great "everyday" dry red wines. The close-neighboring regions of Molise and Puglia also make good

Montepulciano. Since this varietal is highly produced, you'll find everything from generic versions by mass-market companies, to horrible wine, to world-class versions, and our coveted hidden gems.

A good, dry red Montepulciano will hit your mouth with a soft but full body. Then subtle dark cherry and raspberry notes will rise to the top like a swimmer hurrying to break through the water's surface for breath. The fruits are usually subtle with Montepulciano. They won't smack you in the face like California fruit bombs. Montepulciano wines commonly have big round tannins that linger on the finish, but again, it depends on the producer.

There are un-oaked versions that show off a little more fruit for those who like more fruit notes, but some oak-aging with this grape adds more complexity to an otherwise singular flavor profile. The oak adds body and chocolate on the finish. The best Montepulciano wines integrate oak and fruit masterfully.

If you can taste some raspberry and chocolate on the finish, then you've got a winner. If you only taste chocolate, you've got a loser. Montepulciano has a bad reputation for being over-oaked, so knowing the producer is key to finding a hidden gem.

Montepulciano is an age-worthy Italian wine when oaked, but it must be made by a quality producer who hand-selected the grapes.

Catarratto: A white grape that only grows in Sicily. The name is derived from a cataract, or waterfall. The best ones are found in high elevation vineyards like the Madonie Mountains and Mount Etna. The Etna Bianco wine found on the slopes of the volcano in Sicily is part of a blend with its complementary partner, the Carricante grape.

A great Catarratto has a zesty aroma that will take you to a beach on an exotic island where you're lying under the Mediterranean sun, eyes closed, smelling the surrounding lemon trees and hearing the flapping palm trees from the sea breeze. These wines usually have a medium to full body, tropical citrus flavors that makes you thirsty, slippery textures, red apple, and a salt-like minerality.

Barbera: This red grape grows all over Italy, but its best expression comes from the Piemonte region. The two best wines are Barbera d'Asti and Barbera d'Alba. Asti and Alba are two towns in Piemonte, and the Barbera wines that come from them are distinctly different. Barbera d'Alba is more full bodied and smooth while Barbera d'Asti is more wild and lively on the palate. An authentic Barbera has high acidity, grape juice aromas, tingly spices that tickle your gums, forest fruits, and a dry finish with low tannins. The generic Barbera that the Big Wine Industry pushes will be loaded with bitter cherry, oak, and chocolate notes to cover up the wine's defects. Don't fall for it.

Nero d'Avola: The monarch of Sicilian wine. This is the most produced red grape in Sicily. Tasting notes depend on where it's grown on the island. An authentic Nero d'Avola is marked by majestic dark fruits, black pepper, savory spices, and a touch of coffee. The most robust, hot, and bold versions are found in the Western Sections near the Province of Trapani. The more fruit-driven and soft textures come from Central Sicily, and the most structured versions are found in the South Eastern corner. It will be more difficult to find a hidden gem near Trapani because that's where the Big Wine Industry is most concentrated.

Primitivo: Probably the most important grape in the Puglia region. Puglia is a big region, and it produces a ton of this red wine. A great

Primitivo will take you from New World wines to Old World faster than an airplane. The best Primitivo is marked by super juicy and jammy red fruits, syrupy body, cacao, and fruit-filled tannins that will make you suck on your taste buds after the finish. The generic or industrial versions will be highly acidic and have rusty iron tannins. Use the Hidden Gem Formula described later in the book and you'll avoid them. This is a great "transition wine" if you're used to drinking California wines.

Moscato: A sweet wine-lover's dream! Moscato is a sweet white wine, although there are lesser-known red versions. But here, we're talking about sweet white wine. The best version, from Piemonte, is called Moscato d'Asti, but you can also find excellent Moscato in Puglia. Check out Moscato di Trani. The Pugliese version is such a rare wine that a hidden gem is very likely. A good Moscato will be marked with powerful sweet orchard notes: hanging fruits cracking and oozing, apricots, pears, and honey. There is also a sweet and sparkling version called Moscato d'Asti Spumante if you like sweet bubbles.

Negroamaro: This dry red grape is part of an important traditional blend called Salice Salentino. It's a blend of Negroamaro and Malvasia Nera. As a monovarietal, it's best drunk between the ages of two and five years. The best Negroamaro comes from the Salento sub-region. Look for the provinces of Lecce (LE) and Taranto (TA). Don't get concerned if you don't see any province listed, but I'd eliminate the selection if any other provinces are on the back. The best Negroamaro comes from the most southern parts of Puglia. Just look on the front label. You'll usually see Salento IGT.

Negroamaro is an excellent everyday drinking wine. The best

ones are medium bodied and smooth textured, with ripe red forest fruit notes and a touch of earth on the finish. Avoid the over-oaked Big Wine Industry versions. This grape also makes some of the best rosé in Italy. You'll find lots of fresh-cut watermelon and strawberry tart toppings in the Negroamaro rosé. Very refreshing. Even the dry red versions that are lighter-bodied are refreshing if you're looking for an easy red in the summer. Finding a gem for $15 is very possible.

Garganega: This white grape produces some of the best white wines in Italy, found in the Veneto region. The most famous wine made with this grape is called Soave. You're going to have to do some digging at your local wine shop. There will be plenty of generic and Big Wine Industry (BWI) versions.

One of the best dry white wines made with Garganega grapes is called Soave, named after the town of Soave a few miles outside of the city of Verona. When it's made with 100% estate bottled Garganega grapes at a low volume, you'll find a Soave wine marked with mineral, apricot, red apple, and citrus aromas and flavors. This is one of the smoothest and finest white wine in Italy. Generic versions will be astringent, medicinal tasting, and sometimes even rotting fruit.

Trebbiano: This is a white grape used for making dry white wines, and it is found all over Italy. Trebbiano actually has several cousin grapes. One of the best Trebbiano grapes is called Trebbiano Abruzzese; the wine is called Trebbiano d'Abruzzo. Like Garganega, you will find that you're eliminating most of the Trebbiano d'Abruzzo wines off your shopping list because they're made by the BWI. But that's a good thing! We want less choices. An authentic Trebbiano d'Abruzzo is marked with fresh stone fruits and citrus flavors on the nose. They feature comforting texture layers while exuding exciting acidity, and these wines finish with sultry citrus and mineral notes. Finding small wineries that grow Trebbiano is the key for this varietal. More on that in Part 2.

A WORD ABOUT NEBBIOLO

For those of you who are avid Italian wine drinkers, you might be wondering why I didn't include Nebbiolo on the list above. Besides the fact that it's not in the top 10 most produced grapes in Italy, there's another reason: Nebbiolo is a native red grape from Piemonte that makes some of the finest red wines in the world. The most famous Nebbiolo-based wines are Barolo and Barbaresco.

Since it's virtually impossible to find a hidden gem from Barolo or Barbaresco in the $15-$30 price range that I've promised in this book, I've chosen to keep it out. However, you could certainly find a Nebbiolo wine from outside of the Barolo and Barbaresco appellations in our targeted price range. But as you'll see in Part 2, a hidden gem is not solely defined by price.

If you need help finding hidden gems in Barolo and Barbaresco, make sure you sign up for a free account to Hidden Gems so I can let you know when I've published information on this topic.

CHAPTER 13

THE SINGLE BIGGEST CLUE TO FINDING A QUALITY ITALIAN WINE

LONG BEFORE I became an importer, I used to go into wine shops and browse. I loved being surrounded by all the mysterious bottles begging for my attention.

I spent so much time picking up bottles and turning them around to read the back labels that the store managers probably thought I was going to sneak a bottle in my bag and walk out. But I couldn't help myself.

I was fascinated by the diversity of Italian wines. I wanted to know what part of Italy each wine came from and what the wine was made of. If I'd never heard of the town where the winery was located, I'd go home and look it up on the map.

I believe a small part of enjoying a good bottle of Italian wine is also having a sense of where it comes from. Just Italy wasn't good enough. I wanted to know exactly where in Italy the wine was made.

I wanted to learn about the surrounding areas because it might be a place I'd like to visit on vacation sometime.

You never know, maybe there was something historically important or interesting about the area. Maybe the Romans conquered a small tribe in the area of the vineyards because their land was fertile for grape growing. Perhaps the vineyard rests on top of an extinct volcano. In this way, the wine becomes like a time machine because we can't go back, but the grape was there.

The single most important tip I learned in my earlier days of hunting for awesome Italian wines was a two-word phrase: "Estate Bottled."

As a consumer and now as a person in the wine business, there is one important clue that I look for on a bottle of Italian wine that will make or break whether I buy it or not. The single most important requirement I need to be able to justify purchasing a wine is to make sure it is "Estate Bottled." If I don't see these two words on the back label, I'm not buying the wine and neither should you.

If you find an Estate Bottled wine, also make sure that the winery name on the front label is the same company written on the back label. For example, if the winery name on the front label is called "Tenuta Francesco," then somewhere on the back label you should see, "Estate Bottled by Tenuta Francesco." If instead, you see on the back label, "Bottled by Tenuta Francesco," then that means they purchased the grapes somewhere else and bottled the wine themselves. Or, you might see "Estate Bottled by Cantina Antonio" which is a completely different company name. That's a tricky one, but you should also avoid that.

"Estate Bottled" means that the vineyards where the grapes come from and the wine cellar where the wine is made all come from the same property and under the same supervision and ownership. We want to make sure that the integrity of the grape, sub-region, and winemaker are preserved. We can't drink an authentic wine without staying true to the origins of grape, territory, and vine-care.

Estate Bottled designations increase the likelihood that you have a quality product from vine to wine in your hand. That doesn't mean you will like the wine. This is simply one way to help filter your choices down to only authentic wines. I don't want you spending your hard-earned money on generic wines when you can get authentic, hidden gems for the same price or a couple dollars more.

Other Italian wines that I avoid are the ones that were made by a "*Coopertiva.*" A Cooperativa is a group of grape growers, sometimes hundreds, that sell their grapes to a wine house where all the grapes are blended together to make wine. I avoid these wines because you can't taste the essence of a single grape varietal or the place where the wine comes from. When I see the Cooperativa or "Coop." for short, I put the bottle back on the shelf. Just check the back label for those two words. If your budget is $10 for a bottle, then go for it, but this type of wine is not a hidden gem. It's bulk wine in a bottle.

We don't want to support a winery that buys grapes from different farmers. These farmers take care of their land in widely different ways, and the grapes come from different soils and micro climates. Usually the grapes then get thrown on a truck and transported to the winery – sometimes eight hours of travel before arriving at their final destination.

These inconsistencies force the winery to use modern industrial practices to make the wine drinkable. This usually leads to illegitimate wines, full of additives, enzymes, and extra sulfites. There are dozens of additives and interventional technologies that can take bad juice and make it taste like good wine. These wines can also be the cause of those headaches we all complain about.

What's worse is that the non-estate-bottled wineries may charge higher prices for their wines than the small producers! You're probably paying for their marketing budgets.

Occasionally you'll run into Italian wine bottles that never translated the information on the back label. Just in case this happens, I want to give you two examples of estate-bottled wines in Italian so you know what to look for. Both of the following mean "Estate Bottled" in Italian:

- "Prodotto e imbottigliato"

- "Integralmente prodotto e imbottigliato all'origine"

If the bottle writes, "imbottigliato all'orgine" without the word "integralmente," it means that the winery may have bought the grapes and only did the vinification and bottling. It's an industrial practice to maximize a winery's profits. It would be a secondary option for me personally because it's not clear.

When it reads "Prodotto e imbottigliato," it means that the winery both produced the wine and bottled it at the winery. Just like in English, make sure that the company name on the front label is the same name on the back. Otherwise it could be a private label, a topic I discuss in Part 2 called "The Dark Side of the Wine Business."

CHAPTER 14

IMPORTED BY

Have you ever wondered how a wine from Italy makes it to the shelf at a wine shop? The answer is an importer.

The job of an importer is to source wines from foreign countries, manage all the travel logistics to get it to the port, and complete all documentation to pass U.S. Customs. The process is similar no matter which country you live in.

Some boutique wine shops do send their buyers overseas to find their own wines, but an importer still has to bring them to the destination.

The importer name becomes yet another clue that could help us find a hidden gem. When you find a wine that you like, turn the bottle around to see who imported it. Then you can go online and check out the importer's other selections. If it's a small importer, you might discover that you like their taste in wines. It's just another technique to find your next hidden gem.

If you find something in that importer's portfolio that you'd like to try, you can go to wine-searcher.com to see if there are other shops in your area that sell it. Wine-Searcher doesn't show every store in the country that sells a particular bottle of wine, but it's worth taking a quick look. Just don't use it as your sole resource. That would be a big mistake because most stores don't report their inventory to Wine-Searcher. Another thing you can do is ask your local shop if they'll buy a case so you can try it. Get your friends involved and buy a case together.

CHAPTER 15

THE MOST IMPORTANT ITALIAN WORDS TO KNOW

WHEN IT COMES to Italian wines, one big turnoff for people is that all the words on the bottle are in Italian! Just because you can't read or speak Italian doesn't mean you should deny yourself the best wines in the world. Below you'll find a cheat sheet of Italian words that you'll see repeatedly.

There are several words that you will see time and time again when looking at Italian wine labels. After a while, it becomes simply a matter of pattern recognition. These words will demystify many labels. Many Italian producer names begin with the word Cantina, Fattoria, Podere, or Tenuta. This is a clue that you are reading the brand name. There are always exceptions, but a big chunk of wineries use these generic words. Here's a list of the most common words; you should memorize them. You can also go to my YouTube channel called Gladiator Wine TV at https://www.youtube.com/channel/

UCX2azuteOuIvU3z2rLi3PAw where I show you how to pronounce the words in Italian.

Azienda Agricola - Agricultural Company

Biologico - Organic

Biodinamico - Biodynamic

Cantina - This word means "Wine Cellar" in Italian. Many wineries will name their company Cantina ABC which means ABC Wine Cellar. I'll admit it's not a creative name. Usually Cantina is followed by the last name of the family that owns the winery. For example, "Cantina Attanasio."

Cantine - This is the plural version of "cantina" meaning "Wine Cellars." Some wineries name their winery Cantine ABC which means "ABC Wine Cellars." Example: "Cantine Pepi."

Casa Vinicola - Winery or "wine house"

Casa Vitivinicola - Winery or "wine house"

Denominazione di Origine Controllata - Denomination of origin inspected

Denominazione di Origine Controlla e Garantita - Denomination of origin inspected and guaranteed

Feudo - Property

Feudi - Properties

Fattoria - Farm

Fattorie - Farms

Indicazione Geografica Tipica - Typical Geographic Indication

Indicazione Geografica Protetta - Protected Geographic Indication

Denominazione di Origine Protetta - Protected Denomination of Origin

di or d' - of

Podere - Farm

Poderi - Farms

Rosato - Rosé

Società - Partnership

Solfiti - Sulfites

Spumante - Sparkling

Tenuta - This word means "Holding or Estate" in Italian and it's another very common term that wineries will use to name their company. For example, Tenuta ABC means "ABC Estate." Usually Tenuta is followed by the last name of the family that owns the winery. For example, "Tenuta Gallucci."

Tenute - This is the plural version of "tenuta," meaning "Holdings or Estates." Example, Tenute ABC means "ABC Estates." Tenute is usually part of the winery name.

Vino Rosso - Red Wine

Vino Bianco - White Wine

ACTION STEPS:

Here's what you need to do to read the majority of Italian wine labels with ease:

1. Memorize the 20 regions

2. Memorize the top 10 Italian grapes and which regions they come from.

3. Memorize the "town" wine types, the grapes they're made with, and the regions they come from.

4. Memorize The Most Important Italian Words To Know from this chapter.

5. Look for all the words you memorized from steps 1-4 every time you're holding an Italian wine in your hand. That's about 60 Italian words! This should be just enough for you to figure out what types of Italian wine you're looking at.

6. Start sipping and keep a record of every new Italian wine with your phone, Delectable, or Vivino app. Make comparisons between different wine types or grape varietals. Make comparisons between different producers of the same wine type.

7. Remember the Italian wine pyramid. Always think about the grape, region, (sub-region is optional), and producer.

PART 2

The HIDDEN GEM formula

CHAPTER 16

THE HIDDEN GEM FORMULA: INSIDER TIPS FOR CONSUMERS

B<small>Y NOW, YOU</small> know how to read Italian labels, and you have a basic understanding of the classifications, regions, and sub-regions. You also know 10 Italian grapes you should be tasting to form your foundation of Italian wines.

Now we're going deeper into Italian wine. For those of you looking for top class wines in the $15-$30 price range, I've developed the Hidden Gem Formula to help you find those hidden gems.

I developed this browsing method to find amazing wines at affordable prices. I want you to drink like royalty without breaking the bank. While traveling to Italy through the years, I realized that there were so many great wines that never make it to the United States, in part because of the Big Wine Industry.

WHAT'S A HIDDEN GEM?

At the end of the day, a hidden gem is just a matter of opinion. Since my entire business is based on finding hidden gems as a wine importer, I'm going to give you a set of criteria that I use to define a hidden gem. The criteria I use on the wine trails of Italy are the same ones you'll use when shopping for Italian wines in your local area.

A $10 bottle of wine that "tastes good" doesn't in and of itself count as a hidden gem. Since we know that corporate wineries may put additives in the wines to make them taste better, just "tasting good" isn't good enough for us.

As much as I like wine-searcher.com, it's not a good source for finding hidden gems either. It's a place where consumers go to do price comparisons. It's a great tool if you're looking for easier-to-find wines. The only way that wines can appear on Wine-Searcher is if the stores that carry those wines upload them into the database. There are many wine shops that don't work with wine-searcher.

Phone Apps like Vivino are good for reading the opinions of other wine lovers but there are a few issues to take into consideration. One is that you might not have the same taste as the person whose review is influencing your buying decision. You'll also see an "average" price based on their 24 million users around the world. Your area might be above or below that average price.

As a general rule, it's easier to find a hidden gem in the Southern regions of Italy but never rule anything out.

Tip: Download an app on your phone called Delectable. You can use it as your wine diary to compare the wines you've previously enjoyed or despised. Feel free to look me up on Delectable (Tony

Margiotta), because I occasionally write reviews of wines that I try when I'm out to dinner or relaxing at home.

Let's begin with the hidden gem formula below. The first two keys are mandatory. Then you'll see a list of more keys for which you need at least 3 for the wine to be considered a hidden gem. The more keys you have, the more valuable the hidden gem.

A HIDDEN GEM <u>MUST</u> BE:

- **Priced Between $15-$30.** In this price range, we've eliminated the worst of the worst industrial wines and we've eliminated the luxury wines like Barolo. We're looking for a wine that tastes better than the price. Better quality for price. There are many gems to be found in this range, and it's so much fun looking for them!

- **Estate Bottled.** The grapes should have been grown at the same estate as where the winery is located. There should be 100% ownership of all grapes used for winemaking. This ensures consistent quality control and an authentic expression of the soil, climate, and grape that the wine comes from.

A HIDDEN GEM SHOULD CONTAIN <u>AT LEAST 3</u> OF THE FOLLOWING KEYS:

- **Unknown or Lesser-known Brand**. These are brands that only contain the Italian language on the front labels and these are brands that you don't see at every corner wine shop. If it's a brand that you can buy at any store, it's not very hidden. If you walk into five stores in your area, and you see the same brand in all of them, don't even bother.

- **Clearance Sales**. Be cautious with clearance sales. Most of the wines on clearance are some of the worst wines on the planet. Occasionally, a hidden gem gets placed in the clearance section because the store wants to get rid of the inventory. It doesn't hurt to take a look.

- **Small Vineyards.** Ideally we are looking for small wineries that produce no more than 50,000 bottles per year of a single label. This takes research because wine labels rarely print their production numbers on the back labels.

- **Maximum Total Bottle Production.** We are looking for producers whose total bottle production comes under 500,000 bottles per year. That's really where the industrial threshold begins.

- **Hand-Harvested Grapes.** The Big Wine Industry would have you believe that their wines were made by hand-harvested grapes, but they're not. They are machine-harvested. That means the whole harvest happens on the same day; the sour grapes, the infected grapes, the ripe grapes, and the unripe grapes all go back to the cellar for vinification and are treated. Hand-harvesting and even better, hand-selecting grapes is the key to the highest quality of wines.

- **Grape Rarity.** The grapes that we all know like Cabernet Sauvignon, Merlot, Pinot Noir, Pinot Grigio, and Sangiovese are not rare grapes. They're grown all over the world. Look for less-known grape varietals or rare grapes that few regions have. This is one of my favorites!

- **No DOC Associated with the Grape.** If you cannot find a DOC or DOCG for a specific grape varietal, that usually means the grape is rare and doesn't have much history in commercial quantities. Usually an IGT will be associated with it and most likely a small producer is making it.

- **You like the taste.** I'd recommend two books that will teach you how to taste wine: Kevin Zraly's *Windows on the World Wine Course* and Jancis Robinson's *How to Taste.* These books will certainly get you to think about what you're tasting like you never thought possible. In the end, if you've found a hidden gem, it will have to be pleasing to your palate. Keep in mind that some wines you will learn to love slowly as you sit with them and sip. Others you'll love at the first sip. Just keep an open mind.

- **Monovarietal that is Balanced.** Just about any winery with the proper technology and methods can make a blend, with two to five grapes, taste like a complex wine. An artisan who can make a great wine with just a single varietal, especially with a native Italian grape, is a master. A wine made with a single varietal contains 100% of that grape in the bottle. I find that the lesser known grapes produced by industrial wineries make uninteresting versions. Some of these ancient Italian grapes need more love and care to make interesting wines. Hence, the small artisan!

- **Made with Native Grapes.** Since this is a book about hidden Italian wine gems, it must be made with native Italian grapes only. Native Italian grapes will be explained in the next chapter.

CHAPTER 17

NATIVE GRAPES: AUTHENTIC ITALIAN TREASURES

N ATIVE ITALIAN GRAPES have been growing in the same rich soil for at least one thousand years in Italy. Many of them have been growing in Italy for over 2000 years. That's why they are considered native in origin. Calling them "local grapes" might be a more accurate description.

When I spend my money on wine, I want to make sure my wine is authentic. Just tasting "good" isn't good enough for me. Just because a wine comes from Italy doesn't mean that the producers are using native Italian grape varietals. They could be growing international varietals to get a larger piece of the world wine economy.

For example, the infamous "Super Tuscan Wines" are not authentic Italian wines to me because they are blended with three grape varietals: Sangiovese, Cabernet Sauvignon, and Merlot. Only Sangiovese is a native varietal of Italy. The other two grapes are of French origin. So by this logic, it would be difficult to consider this style of wine to be an authentic wine from Tuscany – let alone it being "Super Tuscan"!

In contrast, a wine that is made with 100% Sangiovese grapes would most certainly be a native wine of Italy.

Native Italian wines are important because they have deeply rooted geological ties to the land, soil, climate, and people who cultivate the grapes. They have a history that can be traced back to ancient times and they have a certain historical value to them, just like any artifact in a museum. We should support wineries that make native wines to preserve the rich wine history of Italy. There is no need to chase the next wine trend – like California blends with five grapes or wines aged in bourbon caskets. If you want to experience something new, try the native grapes of Italy. Your palate will love you for it!

These ancient grapes also have distinct characteristics and unique flavors that would be a pity for our palates' pleasure if they didn't exist. Losing these grapes would be like an animal species that goes extinct. We don't want that. We don't want the diverse range of flavors to be destroyed by the Big Wine Industry that wants us to drink the same boring wines forever.

There are more native grapes in Italy than France, Spain, and Greece combined. With an estimated 2,000 native Italian grapes, there are limitless flavors and textures for you to experience. Palate fatigue is impossible!

CHAPTER 18

ISN'T PINOT GRIGIO ITALIAN?

I KNOW. WHEN you're looking for a white wine, Pinot Grigio is the "safe bet." It's always drinkable and easy. You're spending 10 dollars or 20 dollars on what you think is a good one. Are you getting the best white wine for your money?

Probably not.

Here's the deal. Italian wineries know that Pinot Grigio is very popular in the United States and other countries. To take advantage of that popularity, many producers who've never grown Pinot Grigio are now growing it because they can make a lot of money off you.

Even producers in regions that have no history of growing Pinot Grigio grapes are now growing it because the wine has become very trendy.

If you're looking for a hidden gem, whether be it at your local wine shop or online, Pinot Grigio would be the last wine I'd look at.

To even further my point, Pinot Grigio is not an Italian wine. Pinot Grigio comes from Pinot Gris, a French grape. The Italians took the neighboring French grape and made it their own. It's now mostly a mass-produced wine catering to your "safe bet" inclinations.

For 15 to 20 dollars, there are hundreds of hidden gems in Italy you could be swimming in palate pleasure with. In the next section, I'm going to tell you the most secretive key to finding a hidden gem that makes all the difference—and I've already given you the answer a few times!

CHAPTER 19

WHO MAKES HIDDEN GEMS?

Traveling to Italy to visit my relatives in Molise was important to me. To stay connected with the land of my father and my ancestors gave me a sense of identity. For many years during those trips I was surrounded by local wines made by small producers. Some of these wine producers only put out 500 liters per year. At the time, I didn't think anything other than how much I was enjoying the wines. At that time, I missed the most important ingredient to a quality wine: the small producer.

I might not have even fully understood what a small producer was until I went to Sicily to visit a winery in a very obscure territory. The winery was called Castellucci Miano, and they were located high up in the Madonie Mountains. When you think of Sicily, you don't necessarily think about mountains. You think about eggplant parmesan, The Godfather movies, and the Mediterranean Sea. If you're a mountain lover, the Madonie Mountains go up to 6,486 feet at its peak and would make a great place for hiking.

When I went to visit Castellucci Miano, whose vineyards can be found at various altitudes between 500 and 1,000 meters, I began to understand the meaning of the small producer. They have these tiny vineyards, some not much bigger than a suburban backyard in America, where they let the vines grow naturally, without those picturesque rows of vines on wired fences that you see when you go to Napa Valley or Tuscany.

They don't use tractors or machines in the vineyard, which means they practice sustainable agriculture. Everything is taken care of by hand. I remember walking up and down the mountain slopes with Piero Buffa, the director of Castellucci Miano, and noticing that civilization was nowhere in sight. It was just me, Piero, and the grapes. Once you see little vineyards like this in their natural state, you realize that it's impossible to make large quantities of quality wine without machinery.

I was so impressed with the lush, distinct flavors of these wines that I knew I would dedicate my life to supporting the small producer. These wine artisans have a real passion for their land and the fruits that come from it. That passion translates into a wine of distinction. I learned that the key to authentic wine, high quality wine, with distinct flavors and textures, can only be made by the small artisan.

The reason I don't worry too much about the classifications you read about in Part 2 is because I only buy wines from small producers. This is the ultimate key!

Small producers have less land to take care of and they are able to control their vineyards in ways that large producers cannot. For example, a small producer can take care of their vines by hand because they own a few hectares of land, whereas a large producer with 100+ hectares of vine would not be able to take care of their land by hand at all. The large producer is forced to use only heavy machinery to take care of the vineyards because it's not economically feasible to hire an army of workers to take care of the land.

Have you ever seen those vintage charts published by the wine magazines?

They tell you that this year or that year was good for wine. So you look up your little vintage chart and buy wines based on that. The truth is, a small producer will make great wine every year because they know how to salvage their grapes when the weather isn't nice to them.

The large producers unfortunately don't have that luxury. They absolutely must salvage their whole crop, even if it requires chemicals in the vineyards and in the cellar. The photo below shows a small producer hand-harvesting the grapes and an industrial producer harvesting with a machine. Whose wine would you drink?

Small producer hand-harvesting.

Big producer machine-harvesting.

Below are just a few reasons why wines from small producers are better than large producers.

1. Small producers take care of the soil, vines, and grapes by hand. Large producers use machinery.

2. Small producers are able to use less chemicals or no chemicals at all in the vineyards. Large producers are forced to use chemicals like herbicides and pesticides to control and save their vineyards. They commonly use chemical-based fertilizers instead of natural options like green manure.

3. Small producers are capable of sustainable agriculture which means they consume less energy to produce their wine. Sustainable practices are cleaner for the environment and cleaner for the wine.

4. Small producers can hand-pick and hand-select the grapes

during harvest. This means that they can "eyeball" each grape cluster, pick the grapes at the best moment of maturity, and throw away the unhealthy grapes. The large producers collect all the grapes at the same time with machinery and treat the wine using modern intervention practices in the cellar to create consistency and drinkability.

5. If you focus on drinking from small producers, and you find the good ones, you'll never need a vintage chart again. When the climate isn't just right, the small producer knows how to salvage the best of the crop to make a good wine that year. I never look at vintage charts because I don't drink the generic wines from large producers.

6. Small wineries produce a total bottle production of 500,000 bottles of wine per year or less. When you hand-harvest, you really can't produce a lot of wine. But I'm talking about total production, not a single label. I really don't want to see bottle production of more than 100,000 bottles per year for a single label. In theory, a winery could make up to five different types of wines at 100,000 bottles per year each. I prefer much less though. Five hundred thousand bottles per year is really the threshold of where industrialization of wine production begins.

How do you know who is a small producer?

Unfortunately, most labels will never tell you this. Yes, you'll see the occasional "Single Vineyard" description on a front or back label, but if it was made by a mass-market producer, I would personally look elsewhere. They are just trying to profit on customer demand for authentic wines of quality.

In the Italian wine world, there are a few sources that will tell you which wineries are small producers. I've included them in the Resources chapter in the back of this book. Finding small producers is probably the most important aspect to buying authentic Italian wine, but it can be difficult because the labels don't indicate production size.

If you're interested in small producers, make sure you stay in touch with me. I've dedicated my life's work to seeking out the small artisans of Italy. When I have something new to share, you'll be the first to know.

CHAPTER 20

PRIVATE LABELS: THE DARK SIDE OF THE WINE BUSINESS

SOME WINERIES PRODUCE so much wine that they can't sell it all under their own brand name. So they create "private labels": a completely different brand that contains the same exact wine. Sometimes the retail price is higher, sometimes lower. Either way, it's certainly possible to walk into a wine shop where two completely different bottles of wine contain the same exact wine!

HERE'S HOW TO AVOID PRIVATE LABELS:

Look on the front label and find the name of the winery. For example, "Cantina Emilio" is on the front label. When you go to look at the back label, you should see something like "Estate bottled by Cantina Emilio" or "Produced by Cantina Emilio." If you see "Cantina Emilio" on the front label but you see "Bottled by Tenuta

Terre Buone" on the back label, then it's probably a private label and you should not buy it.

Another clue is a wine with a catchy title on the front like, "Tuscan Skies" and the name of the producer is nowhere to be found on the front label. That bottle probably doesn't exist in Italy and was made for export only. I avoid wines like that because I feel like the corporate Big Wine Industry is taking me for a ride. That same wine, "Tuscan Skies," is probably a table wine somewhere in Italy for 1.50 Euros a liter. And I get it. If you can only afford a $10 bottle of wine, and it happens to be a private label, by all means, enjoy! But in this book, we're hunting for hidden gems.

Here's another one. You find a Barolo for $20 at the wine shop. It's either a terrible wine or a private label. You'll never find a quality Barolo at that price point. This also brings us back to the "cooperative" that I was telling you about before. It's the group of grape growers that sell their grapes to a central winery that mixes them all and makes cheap wine with them. Imagine how many "brands" a cooperativa can create. Same juice but different labels. For a hidden gem seeker, this is like discovering a copy or a fake.

If we avoid these wines, producers will eventually listen. We want more quality for our money and this would force them to do so. From my experience, Italian producers are making better and better wine each year. The techniques and practices are getting more refined. I have no doubt that Italy has the capability to increase the quality for the price range we're discussing in this book as we move forward into the future while other wine regions of the world will not be able to compete. The Italian soil, grape, and climate are the fundamentals that no country on Earth can copy.

CHAPTER 21

THE TRUTH ABOUT
90 POINT SCORES

J UST ABOUT EVERY store you walk into, you'll see either a card in front of a bottle that shows "90 Points!" or you'll see an entire section at the store with a huge sign that writes "90+ Wines under $20."

All of these wines were given 90 points or more by various wine magazines. These publications have a team of wine critics who apparently blindfold themselves, taste wines, write a review, and give a score from 50-100. Whichever bottles get 90 points usually sell more because people trust these publications and don't want to invest time in learning anything about wine.

Those of us with the passion for Italian wine, like me and you, should invest a little time to make our own buying decisions.

I don't want to badmouth the wine magazines because great wines can be found in them, but it is a pay-to-play system. For example, if you're a big brand winery, that makes millions of bottles per year, you probably have a marketing budget. So you take some money, give it to a wine publication for an advertisement page, and then you coincidentally get a 95-point score and you sell more wine and at a higher price. While there isn't any hard evidence of this, it's simple math. How can any magazine, whether wine-related or not, have enough money to pay for its operations and employees, and also make a profit? The answer is advertising. If I own a big winery and I buy a page of advertising in a wine magazine, I'm going to expect a high score for my wine. Do you think I'll buy another advertisement if my wine gets a low score? Think about it.

When you buy one of these wines, you're actually giving extra money to the winery so that they can continue to target advertisements towards you. You're paying them to advertise to *you*.

Many wine store owners that I know don't think the 100-point system is legitimate either. Some resist it at their own risk, and others continue to buy and support those "90-point" wines. My advice is to help retail stores help you. Ask them for small producers and they will gladly help you. If they don't, be persistent or find a store that will accommodate your request.

CHAPTER 22

WINE HEADACHES EXPLAINED

L ET ME BEGIN by saying that I'm not a doctor and I'm not giving any medical advice. Nothing in this book is medical advice and you should always speak with your doctor before you try my suggestions. If you have some sort of allergy or diagnosis that prevents you from drinking red or white wine, then my suggestions probably won't help.

Have you ever gotten that dreaded headache from a night of drinking red wine? Or any type of wine like white or rosé for that matter.

We've all had it. Do you know what the media has blamed? The sulfites. From my experience and speaking with artisans in Italy, I don't believe that this common phenomenon is necessarily the root cause of the headache. Although it's still on the table as a possible cause.

Artisans in Italy have told me that the most common reason for the wine headache is because we are drinking blends — that is wines made with at least two different grape varietals and more likely three to five different grapes.

We don't have any science to back up these claims to my knowledge, but the farmers and artisans that work the land know their wines on a more intimate level than we'll ever know. It's worth an experiment at the minimum.

What I suggest is you look for what we call a mono-varietal wine. This is a wine made with a single grape. So if you buy a Sangiovese, I would have to be assured by the winery that it's made with 100% Sangiovese grapes. Not 90% Sangiovese and 10% Cabernet Sauvignon like the Super Tuscans.

I'd also recommend you read a book called *The Wine Savant* by Michael Steinberger. It's an easy-to-read book about the wine culture of today. Savant explains how wineries are putting strange additives into their wines such as enzymes, wood chips, and other artificial flavors to make their commercial wines more approachable to drink. These additives are not mandatory ingredients to be reported on the back labels. Only sulfites are mandatory on the back label and that's why sulfites are attacked as the reason for the wine headache.

With that said, I would still look for wines made with a lower amount of sulfites. I've been told by artisans that the average commercial bottle of wine contains upwards of 120 mg of sulfites per liter. I'm satisfied with any wine that comes in below that number. If you buy wines that claim 0 sulfites, I'd drink them within the first year of release because after that, the wine may not be good for drinking anymore. Bacteria could ruin it.

Along with small producers, this is another difficult piece of info that's hard to obtain. The only way is to write to the producer and ask for the precise amount of sulfites per liter. Keep in mind that a normal size bottle of wine contains 3/4 of a liter, or 750 milliliters.

CHAPTER 23

DESTRUCTION OF ITALIAN WINE MYTHS

CHIANTI AND PINOT GRIGIO ARE THE ONLY ITALIAN WINES.

THIS MIGHT SEEM ridiculous if you know anything about Italian wines. But there are people who only drink the most common wine types: Cabernet, Merlot, Pinot Noir, etc. When it comes to Italian wines, these drinkers' imaginations are limited to the clichéd bottle of Chianti covered in straw sitting on top of a red and white checkered table at an Italian restaurant.

Pinot Grigio isn't even a native Italian wine. It grows very well in Italy, and the wine is always easy and drinkable. It got popular because of millions of dollars in marketing and pushing the product so that it became a household name. Again, you didn't find that Pinot Grigio, it found you!

ITALIAN WINES USUALLY HAVE UNPLEASANT FLAVORS LIKE TAR, TOBACCO, DUSTINESS, AND VINEGAR.

This is an overgeneralization. With over 2,000 different grape varietals, and thousands of registered wineries in Italy, there is a flavor for everyone. Anything you're looking for, there is an Italian wine that will fulfill your need. The Hidden Gem Formula will help you narrow it all down so you can find that hidden gem that will debunk the myth.

I'd also like to say that if you only drink California wines, then many wines from the Mediterranean might seem vinegary or tart because those "Cali-wines" are loaded with sugar. I'm sorry to say, but you're kind of drinking an alcoholic soda. That doesn't mean you should force yourself to drink something you don't like. Just keep looking and tasting!

ITALIAN WINES ARE ONLY GOOD WITH FOOD.

While culturally, yes, the Italians have made their local wines to be paired with their local cuisines, a lot has changed in the wine world of Italy lately. It is getting easier to find "cocktail wines," which are wines that you can drink without food and experience great palate pleasures. For "cocktail wine" recommendations, read the next chapter, the Top Ten "Cocktail" Wines in Italy.

ITALIAN WINES ARE TOO ACIDIC.

This is what people say when they feel that "burning" sensation on their front tongue or that "cutting" sensation when they swallow a wine. This is a good thing, but the degree is what's important. Yes, too much is bad. But acidity that is balanced with the flavor of the wine and the tannins is what brings liveliness to the wine. Too little acidity will taste flat and boring in your mouth. Some Italian grapes produce more acidity than others. Again, with so many varietals to choose from, you can find any Italian wine that suits your sensitivity to acidity.

ALL THE GOOD ITALIAN WINES ARE EXPENSIVE.

The whole point of this book is to destroy this myth. Yes, the great Italian wines like Barolo, Barbaresco, and Brunello have a high price tag. But there are hundreds of hidden gems outside of those three wines, waiting for you to discover. Many of which are just as good, or even better than the wines just mentioned. For those of you who are big fans of those pricey wines above, I promise you that I will dedicate a completely separate project to find the hidden gems in their category. Putting the "3 B's" aside, the "sweet spot" for hidden gems is $15-$30. If you can afford that price range, you can drink like royalty if you use the Hidden Gem Formula.

BAROLO, BARBARESCO, AND BRUNELLO ARE THE BEST ITALIAN WINES.

Just because all the wine critics write about these wines doesn't mean they're the best. Keep tasting and keep trying different types of wines. You might discover something that gives your palate more pleasure than these wines. The best Italian wine is ultimately your choice.

You don't need to be a wine expert to develop your own palate. When you drink a bottle of wine, you'll know if you like or don't like it. The more you taste and the more you try different grape varietals and different producers, you'll learn more about wine and about yourself. What moves you? What pleases your senses?

You'll know you've experienced a great bottle of wine when you feel sad because the bottle is empty. There are many wines that are so exciting when you have that first glass, but after that glass or two, you become fatigued or bored of the wine. That happens frequently and is a simple indicator that you're drinking an industrial wine.

CHAPTER 24

THE TOP 10 "COCKTAIL WINES" OF ITALY

A "COCKTAIL WINE" is an easy-to-drink wine that you can have without food. Maybe it's something you drink when friends come over. Maybe it's something you start drinking while you're cooking a nice meal. Maybe it's a "TV Wine," something you drink after dinner while you watch TV before bedtime. These wines taste nothing like a cocktail. These are all normal wines between 12-14% alcohol. We're calling these "cocktail wines" simply because they are easy wines to drink anytime. All the wines on the list below are native Italian wines, listed in no particular order. I'd also note that the wines below are also good with food.

A "cocktail wine" should be more fruit driven, with a soft finish. These wines are not bitter nor astringent. Some of these will be harder to find than others.

These are not the only cocktail wines. The producer is always more important than both the vintage and the grape which means that other types of Italian wines would make great cocktail wines under the supervision of a particular winemaker. A great producer can take a grape that is harsh or bitter and turn it into a mouthwatering masterpiece.

1. Prosecco (white sparkling), Veneto

2. Vermentino (dry white), Sardegna

3. Primitivo (dry red), Puglia

4. Cerasuolo d'Abruzzo (dry rosé), Abruzzo

5. Pecorino (dry white), Abruzzo

6. Nerello Mascalese (red), Sicily

7. Lambrusco (red sparkling), Emilia-Romagna

8. Recioto (sweet red), Veneto

9. Frappato (dry red), Sicily

10. Falanghina (dry white), Campania

CHAPTER 25

WHY NOT START
A WINE CLUB?

NOTHING IS MORE fun than sharing wine with friends. Drinking wine with friends creates a natural bond. It also creates a relaxed learning environment to talk about the wines and exchange opinions. With so many Italian wines out there to experience, a quick and fun way to expand your knowledge is to get a bunch of friends together and create an Italian wine club.

Get a group together, no more than 12 people, to meet once a month to go over different Italian wines. You could do one Italian region per month and select the most common varietals from each region. Or you do an Italian Reds night where each person brings a bottle of wine that retails for $20, cover up the labels, and vote on the best one. Then reveal the winner at the end of the tasting. You might discover a varietal that you really like or a producer that you think is brilliant.

You could also use your club as a tactic to get the best discounts at a wine shop. If you'll be meeting once a month, tell the wine shop owner that you'd like to buy a mixed case of wine every month and ask what kind of discount you can get. If you don't like the offer, go to another store.

You could easily taste 12 new grape varietals a year while having quality social time with like-minded friends.

If you need help getting some "hidden gem" wine recommendations for your wine club, you can get your first recommendation for FREE at http://www.gladiatorwine.com/hiddengems

PART 3

HOW TO SHOP FOR ITALIAN WINES

CHAPTER 26

THE VALUE PLAY: ITALIAN REGIONS WITH THE BEST VALUE FOR YOUR MONEY

THE WINES OF North Italy, from Tuscany and up, generally cost more than their southern counterparts. I recommend you start your hidden gem searches in three regions: Abruzzo, Puglia, and Sicily. They make delicious wines that are competitively priced.

We will delve into all three regions and break down which types of wines you should be looking for.

CHAPTER 27

VALUE PLAY 1: ABRUZZO

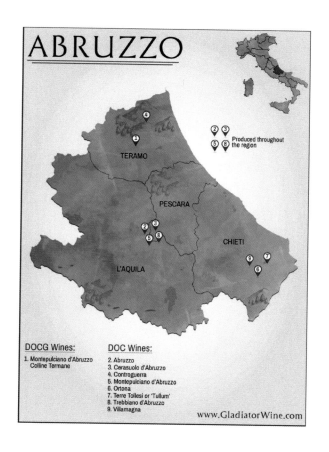

ABRUZZO

TERAMO

PESCARA

CHIETI

L'AQUILA

② ③
⑤ ⑧ Produced throughout
the region

DOCG Wines:

1. Montepulciano d'Abruzzo
   Colline Termane

DOC Wines:

2. Abruzzo
3. Cerasuolo d'Abruzzo
4. Controguerra
5. Montepulciano d'Abruzzo
6. Ortona
7. Terre Tollesi or 'Tullum'
8. Trebbiano d'Abruzzo
9. Villamagna

www.GladiatorWine.com

THE REGION OF Abruzzo is attached to Molise, which happens to be the region where my family is from. Many decades ago Abruzzo and Molise were part of the same region: Abruzzo-Molise. This used to create confusion among the people that lived there. People who were born when the region was connected all considered themselves *Abruzzesi*, while the generations after the separation identified themselves based on the border.

I can remember as a little boy when my grandmother and my father used to argue in Italian dialect about *what they were*. My grandmother used to shout at my dad in Italian with that famous one arm swinging up and down, "Siamo Abruzzesi! (We're Abruzzesi), and my dad would shout back, "No! Siamo Molisani! (No! We're from Molise!). It was always funny to watch them argue over such a silly thing.

Abruzzo is found on the Adriatic Sea. It's a very "hilly" region with a massive mountain range called the Appennini. These mountains typically have snow even in the summer. If you like nature and hiking, it's worth a trip.

Red Wine in Abruzzo

In Abruzzo, look for a type of wine called Montepulciano d'Abruzzo. For $15-20 you can usually find some excellent versions for an everyday low price. The challenge is that there are many brands that make this wine.

So how do you find the good ones in that price range? Use the Hidden Gem Formula that you learned in Part 2 of this book.

WHITE WINES IN ABRUZZO

Trebbiano is one of the most common white grapes in Italy. I usually cook with this wine because it's cheap and you'll rarely find a good one at your wine shop. It's usually blended with other grapes to make cheap table wine. Trebbiano grapes grow all over Italy with varying results but Trebbiano d'Abruzzese is one of the best.

Even with Trebbiano d'Abruzzo, you'll still need a small producer who cultivates the grape by hand if you're looking for a good one. This will require some research because there are so many brands that make this wine. That's where the Hidden Gem Formula comes into play.

There are two other white grapes from Abruzzo that are worth investigating: Passerina and Pecorino. Since these grapes are less known, you'll have better success at finding a hidden gem on your first try. You're looking at $15 - $20 for these quality white wines.

I love Pecorino. It's one of the first white wines that I got exposed to when visiting my family in Molise. It's more common to find Pecorino from Abruzzo when you're shopping in the U.S. but Molise Pecorino is also very good. It's usually packed with some refreshing stone fruit notes and reinvigorating minerality. Passerina can be quite a sophisticated white wine with citrus and tropical fruit notes.

CHAPTER 28

VALUE PLAY 2: PUGLIA

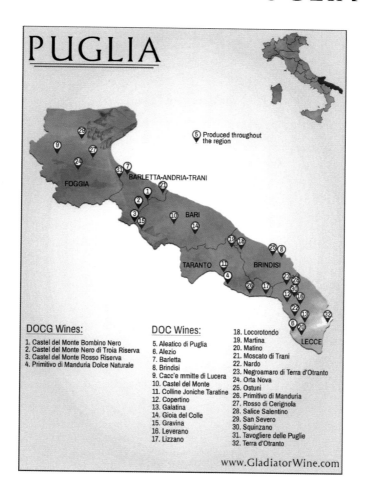

PUGLIA

⑤ Produced throughout the region

BARLETTA-ANDRIA-TRANI

FOGGIA

BARI

TARANTO

BRINDISI

LECCE

DOCG Wines:
1. Castel del Monte Bombino Nero
2. Castel del Monte Nero di Troia Riserva
3. Castel del Monte Rosso Riserva
4. Primitivo di Manduria Dolce Naturale

DOC Wines:
5. Aleatico di Puglia
6. Alezio
7. Barletta
8. Brindisi
9. Cacc'e mmitte di Lucera
10. Castel del Monte
11. Colline Joniche Taratine
12. Copertino
13. Galatina
14. Gioia del Colle
15. Gravina
16. Leverano
17. Lizzano
18. Locorotondo
19. Martina
20. Matino
21. Moscato di Trani
22. Nardo
23. Negroamaro di Terra d'Otranto
24. Orta Nova
25. Ostuni
26. Primitivo di Manduria
27. Rosso di Cerignola
28. Salice Salentino
29. San Severo
30. Squinzano
31. Tavogliere delle Puglie
32. Terra d'Otranto

www.GladiatorWine.com

O NE OF MY favorite regions in Italy, Puglia is the "heel" of the "Italian boot." On the inside of the heel you'll find the Ionian Sea, and on the outside of it you'll find the Adriatic Sea.

When I go to Puglia, I typically go to the Ionian Sea side (which I personally think is more beautiful). The food is amazing no matter which side you're on. I don't want to get too far off topic, but Puglia has the best food-to-price ratio in Italy. I eat like a king there and spend very little.

While tourists are sweating like pigs taking tours of Rome, I prefer to be laying on the beach gazing beyond my feet at the gorgeous blue hues of the Ionian Sea. Then at night I'll go to an "agriturismo" where you can find some of the best food in the area. These are little farms with their own restaurants where you can experience what actual fresh food tastes like.

Puglia is a massive wine region worth exploring. There are many native grape varietals and many sub-regions. It's also the home of some amazing wines at great prices. Let's begin.

RED WINE IN PUGLIA

Puglia is a wonderful region for rich, juicy, and succulent red wines. Primitivo or Negroamaro are great value choices for reds; they both have beautiful rich red fruit notes and savory finishes. They make great everyday wines. There is also a traditional red blend called Salice Salentino that is made of two native grapes: Negroamaro and Malvasia Nera.

You can find great red wines from Puglia in the $15-$25 range.

If you follow the Hidden Gem Formula from Part 2, you'll discover wines from the region that cost $17-20 and are more profound than that $30 Cab you bought from California. Primitivo, in particular, makes a great "transition wine" if you typically drink California reds and want to get into Italian wine.

CHAPTER 29

VALUE PLAY 3: SICILY

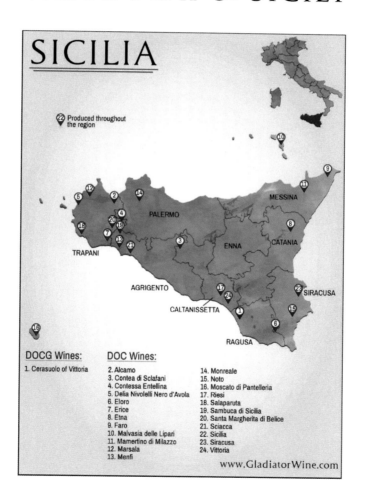

SICILIA

22 Produced throughout the region

MESSINA

PALERMO

TRAPANI

ENNA

CATANIA

AGRIGENTO

SIRACUSA

CALTANISSETTA

RAGUSA

DOCG Wines:
1. Cerasuolo of Vittoria

DOC Wines:
2. Alcamo
3. Contea di Sclafani
4. Contessa Entellina
5. Delia Nivolelli Nero d'Avola
6. Eloro
7. Erice
8. Etna
9. Faro
10. Malvasia delle Lipari
11. Mamertino di Milazzo
12. Marsala
13. Menfi
14. Monreale
15. Noto
16. Moscato di Pantelleria
17. Riesi
18. Salaparuta
19. Sambuca di Sicilia
20. Santa Margherita di Belice
21. Sciacca
22. Sicilia
23. Siracusa
24. Vittoria

www.GladiatorWine.com

SICILY IS THE thumping-heart of the Mediterranean, Italy's largest wine region with an endless array of grape varietals. Winemaking can be traced back over 2,500 years on the island, but Sicily has only recently been having a wine renaissance.

One time, I found myself in Taormina, a small seaside town on the eastern coast of Sicily. I was taking a small vacation before my appointments with some wineries. What's interesting about this town is that most of the village rests on top of a mountain; if you stay up in the mountain, you'll have breathtaking views of the Mediterranean Sea and Mount Etna, the largest active volcano in Europe.

So one night in Taormina, I walked over to their old city section to a pizzeria that was recommended to me. While I was having pizza, I got into a conversation about wine with the waiter. I was drinking a Nerello Mascalese – a native grape that grows on the slopes of Mount Etna – and I was expressing how much I was enjoying it.

The waiter then began telling me about his favorite wine in the whole world, which of course was Sicilian. I was surprised that he knew about this particular wine because it's very rare. I won't mention the wine in this book because its price tag is too high, but the point of the story is that wine is taken so seriously in Sicily that even waiters at a pizzeria know their wines intimately.

The best part about Sicilian wine is that there is something for everyone at any price. Let's get started with the Sicilian Value Plays.

WHITE WINE IN SICILY

Sicily is one of my favorite wine regions in Italy and the home of some great white wines. Look for Catarratto or Grillo; you can find good ones between $15-20. Also look for Etna Bianco, a white blend of

Catarratto and Carricante grapes found on the slopes of the Mount Etna Volcano. These wines used to be very expensive, but many have come down in price in recent years while others remain pricey. You can find a hidden gem for $20! It's guaranteed to shock your palate with its rich volcanic mineral notes.

RED WINE IN SICILY

Nero d'Avola is the monarch of red wine in Sicily. It can vary greatly depending on where it was made on the island. While you can find many Nero d'Avola bottles for $10, I'd stay away unless that's all you can afford. If you see the letters (TP) on the back label, and it costs $10, it's probably an industrial wine. The (TP) stands for Province of Trapani, the most industrial zone of the wine market in Sicily. The odds are high that you're not getting a good value. I have nothing against the wines of Trapani, but it would require a lot of research to dig through all those wines to find a hidden gem. This is a great example of the Map Technique I discussed in an earlier chapter.

With that said, Nero d'Avola is a delicious wine that goes really well with food. It can be robust or light and fruity.

If you can find a Cerasuolo di Vittoria, you should be able to find a hidden gem for $20-$25. This wine is a blend of Nero d'Avola and Frappato combining robust and light flavors. When it hits your mouth, you feel the lightness and bright cherry fruits. As the wine moves to your mid-palate, the body builds and develops darker fruits as the Nero d'Avola reveals itself. The finish is dry, with mixed berries and earth. A blend with a distinguished history and a rare gem that few outside of Sicily know about, Cerasuolo di Vittoria happens to be the only DOCG classification in Sicily.

CHAPTER 30

BEST ROSÉ IN ITALY

WHETHER YOU LOVE or hate rosé, you should check out Puglia, Italy's "Land Of Rosé." There are two grapes you should look for in the Puglia section: Bombino Nero and Negroamaro.

A Bombino Nero Rosé or *Rosato* in Italian is the only DOCG rosé in Italy. It's very difficult to find, but when you do, it's almost guaranteed to be a hidden gem. You might have to special order it. It's super savory and bright, with notes of lush red fruits, crispy acidity, and a fuller body.

In Abruzzo, look for Cerasuolo d'Abruzzo. It's considered the best rosé in Italy, but it tastes totally different from the rosé in Puglia. Made with Montepulciano grapes, it's a much deeper pink than the rosé from Puglia. Its common characteristics are dried red cherries on the front with candy notes on a dry finish. The Puglia rosé are more watermelon and strawberry-focused with dry and savory finishes.

It's a misnomer that darker pink rosé means they are sweet. You'll notice that both Cerasuolo d'Abruzzo and the rosé from Puglia have a deeper pink than the trendy clear rosé of late. Trust me, these deeper colored rosé are dry, salivating, and profound.

CHAPTER 31

ITALIAN BUBBLES

IF YOU EVER walk into a bar or convenience store in Italy, you will see that there are more sparkling water bottles on the shelf than natural water bottles. That's because Italians love their bubbles; many Italians will tell you it's for good digestion. Sparkling wines are also super popular in Italy.

There are three main types of Italian sparkling wine: Prosecco, Spumante, and Francia Corta.

Prosecco is the most popular sparkling white wine. You can find everything from $10-$30, which makes selecting one difficult. Make sure the Prosecco is a DOC or DOCG from Veneto. If the label says Prosecco and you don't see either of those classifications, it's probably a fraudulent one.

Spumante is a style of sparkling wine made with almost any grape. Some of my favorite Spumante are made with Pecorino and Falanghina. There are even Rosé Spumante if you enjoy both bubbles and rosé. Historically, spumante wines were considered cheap and low quality. All that has changed with Italy's increase in quality throughout the whole country. Some spumante's are really exceptional now.

Francia Corta is considered one of the best sparkling wines in the world. This wine is often compared to the finest champagne of France. Make sure your credit card is fresh for this one. You would be spending outside of our target $15-30 dollar range. Francia Corta is too expensive to be a hidden gem, but you should know that it exists.

CHAPTER 32

IF YOU LIKE THIS, TRY THAT!

I've hosted wine tastings for thousands of people all around New York. One of the most common questions I get when doing an Italian wine tasting is: "What can you compare this wine to?" or "How does it compare to a Merlot?"

I'm sure many of you have had famous French and Californian wines like Cabernet, Pinot Noir, and Chardonnay. I put the below two infographics together to compare these famous international wines with native Italian wines. For example, while a Sauvignon Blanc does not taste exactly like a Vermentino, they both share a crisp acidity. It's a fun way to begin exploring native Italian wines and expanding your palate.

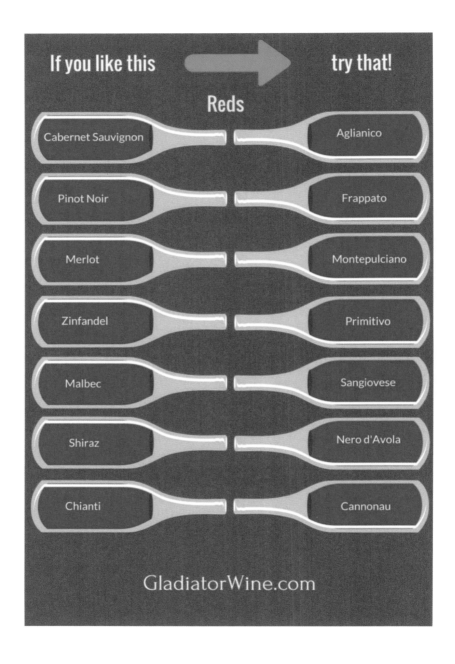

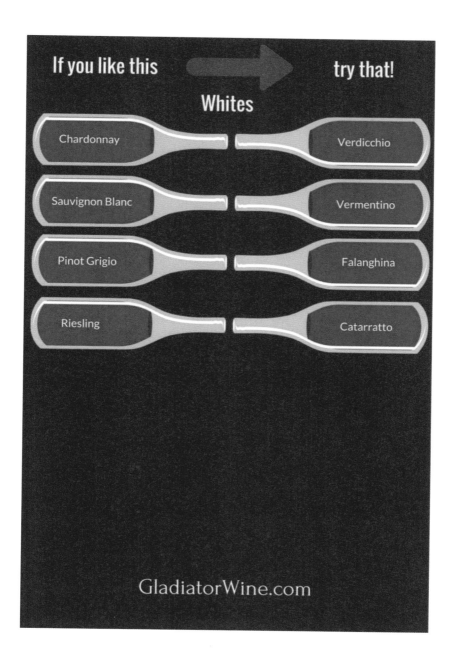

CHAPTER 33

ONLINE SHOPPING FOR ITALIAN WINE

S HOPPING FOR WINE online is getting better. There are certainly more selections available online than there were just five years ago, even though most of these selections are mass-market or generic wines that we're trying to avoid.

Is it possible to find a hidden gem from Italy online? The short answer is yes. The ease of finding a hidden gem will depend on where you live. Never give up though. A hidden gem may be waiting patiently for you in the corner.

The first thing you should do is a local search on Google for "online wine" and where you live. You want to start with brick and mortar stores near you that have online stores. They will deliver wines to your door the quickest.

If you live in the U.S., you can also look for online stores that will ship to your state. The online stores that I'm recommending below are U.S. based stores. If you live in another country, the Hidden Gem Formula will still work in your local wine store and online. If you're not living in the U.S. you can still do your research on the websites below because some of them do ship internationally.

BELOW IS A LIST OF ONLINE RETAILERS, SOME OF WHICH HAVE A BRICK AND MORTAR STORE:

http://www.corksoncolumbus.com - Corks on Columbus is an excellent boutique shop near Central Park in New York City. Top-notch service, easy-to-use online store, and hidden gems can be found there. They ship to most states.

Highly recommended: https://shop.royalwinemerchants.com - Royal Wine Merchants is a little boutique shop in downtown Manhattan. They have an excellent selection of gems, their staff is very knowledgeable, and they ship quickly. They ship to most states.

http://www.sokolin.com - Boutique online wine store based in New York. Houses some Italian hidden gems, and they ship out of state. Make sure you check which states they ship to before buying.

http://www.wine.com - When you go to their site, make sure you choose which state you live in before you start browsing because your options and prices will adjust according to your state. This the largest online store in the U.S. While most of the selections are generic, hidden gems can be found on their site. Browse periodically to see if any hidden gems show up.

http://www.totalwine.com - Ships wine to many states. Most of their selections are mass-market, but if you periodically do a search on their site, you can find a hidden gem. Their wine catalog is enormous since they are one of the largest retailers in the U.S. Also, check periodically to see if they added your state for shipping.

INTERNATIONAL SHIPPING

http://www.klwines.com - Opportunities for hidden gems are lurking on this site. Ships internationally to Hong Kong, Japan, and South Korea. Also ships to most states. Check periodically to see if your state has been added.

http://www.sothebyswine.com - If you live outside of the Unites States, Sotheby's Wine will ship internationally. All you have to do is write to them and ask them for a shipping quote. Click on their shipping policy to get more info: http://ny.sothebyswine.com/shipping.cfm

CHAPTER 34

HOW TO NAVIGATE
THE WINE SHOP

NOW THAT YOU know the names of the regions in Italy, the classifications, 10 Italian wine grapes, how to read labels, and the Hidden Gem Formula...it's time to go shopping!

THERE ARE 3 TYPES OF WINE SHOPS:

1. Boutique Wine Shops - These are small stores that specialize in quality wines. They will have knowledgeable staff to help make recommendations, and they usually have a good selection of small, estate-bottled wineries to choose from.

2. Generic Liquor Stores - These stores carry the generic wine brands like Yellowtail, Cupcake, Mondavi, Apothic, Ruffino, Corvit, and Santa Margherita. These stores are found everywhere. They are usually very "old" looking and seem like they haven't been cleaned in 50 years.

But watch out, there are new generic liquor stores that open all the time. They might put in shiny hardwood floors and spotlights in the ceiling, but these stores are no different from their "older" cousins because they still carry the same old brands. They want to give the appearance of being boutique while selling generic wines.

3. Wine Chain Stores - These are usually really big stores that have multiple locations. They carry all the big, mass-market brands at the most competitive prices. Going into a store like this and finding a hidden gem is possible if you're up for the challenge.

You can visit all of these stores in search of a hidden gem. The Boutique Wine Shops will probably carry several hidden gems because it's their job to do so, but the other two might have some surprises at a competitive price.

IN WINE SHOPS, THERE ARE USUALLY TWO WAYS THAT ITALIAN WINES ARE ORGANIZED:

1. Some stores will just display an "Italy" sign.

2. Other stores have the "Italy" display but then place smaller signs designating the various regions. For example, "Tuscany" or "Piedmont."

I personally prefer the regional separation because it helps me filter down to what I'm looking for in a much faster way.

When it comes to thinking about Italian wines, I organize them in my mind by region and by grape varietal. If you're new to Italian wines, take it easy. This is your new hobby. Embrace it and it will develop naturally.

I'm not going to tell you that one region in Italy is better than the other. I love them all! As you get to know Italian wines more, you'll use these regional display signs in wine shops to help you find what you're looking for.

Once you've arrived at the Italian section, you've got to choose a region. The most common Italian wine regions you'll see are: Piedmont, Tuscany, Abruzzo, and Sicily. You'll find wines from these regions in just about any wine shop. If you see even more regions displayed in the store, your chances increase greatly that there's a hidden gem waiting for you. Displaying more regional signs than the usual suspects above is a sign that the store highly values Italian wines and invests great efforts to give customers an authentic Italian experience.

I find that the best deals are in Abruzzo, Sicily, and Puglia. To find a good bottle of wine from Piemonte or Tuscany, you'll expect to pay $30 and up. If I can find a world class wine from these regions between $20-$30, I'd consider it a gem. If you find a $15 bottle from Piemonte, it's probably to be avoided.

CHAPTER 35

THE FERRARI FAST CHEAT SHEET

I REALIZE SOME people won't have the patience to read the whole book when you are making your selections in a wine store. What follows is a super-fast cheat sheet to help you shop for Italian wine quickly. This quick guide will help you quickly filter out the obvious mass market wines, but it won't necessarily help you find a hidden gem.

I'VE BROKEN THE CHEAT SHEET INTO FOUR SECTIONS:

Red Wine $15-20, White Wine $15-20, Red Wine $20-30, and White Wine $20-30.

For free visual examples, sign up for Hidden Gems and I'll send them to you: http://www.gladiatorwine.com/hiddengems

Now, let's hit the gas pedal!

CHAPTER 36

RED WINE $15-$20

FIVE CHECKMARKS TO BUYING QUALITY ITALIAN RED WINE

1. Look for Abruzzo or Sicily in your wine shop's Italian section. These are two regions in Italy, and there should be separate signs for each. If not, ask the wine shop's manager to show you which wines come from these regions in this price range.

2. Look for Montepulciano d'Abruzzo or Nero d'Avola. Montepulciano is from the Abruzzo region, and Nero d'Avola is from Sicily. The wine type is usually found on the front label, the back label, or on both.

3. Make sure the name of the winery, which is printed on the front label, has the same company name on the back. Avoid wines with different company names on the front and back label.

4. Make sure you see the words "Estate Bottled" on the back label. "Bottled by" is not good enough.

5. Avoid wines that have the word "Coop" or "Cooperativa" on the back label.

CHAPTER 37

WHITE WINE $15-$20

FIVE CHECKMARKS TO BUYING QUALITY ITALIAN WHITE WINE

1. Look for Campania or Abruzzo. Look for a sign in the Italian section that shows Campania. If not, ask the wine shop manager to show you which wines come from these regions in this price range.

2. Look for Falanghina, Fiano, or Pecorino. Fiano and Falanghina can be found in Campania, and Pecorino can be found in Abruzzo. The wine type might be found on the front label, the back label, or on both.

3. Make sure the name of the winery, which is printed on the front label, has the same company name on the back. Example: "Cantina Giusto" is the name of the company on the front label. On the back label, it should say "Estate bottled by Cantina Giusto." You might see Cantina Giusto written

on the top of the back label and the words "Estate Bottled" written somewhere else on the back; that's acceptable.

4. Make sure you see the words "Estate Bottled" on the back label. Don't buy it if it just says "Bottled by…"

5. Avoid wines that have the word "Coop" or "Cooperativa" on the back label. It's usually found in the sentence where it says "Bottled by Coop…" or "Produced by Cooperativa…"

CHAPTER 38

RED WINE $20-$30

FIVE CHECKMARKS TO BUYING QUALITY ITALIAN RED WINE

1. Look for Sicily or Puglia in your wine shop's Italian section. These are two regions in Italy, and there should be separate signs for each. If not, ask the wine shop manager to show you which wines come from these regions in this price range.

2. Look for Perricone, Etna Rosso, or Primitivo di Manduria or Primitivo Salento. These are types of red wine. Perricone and Etna Rosso are from Sicily and Primitivo is from Puglia. The wine type might be found on the front label, the back label, or on both.

3. Make sure the name of the winery, which is printed on the front label, has the same company name on the back. Example: "Cantina Giusto" is the name of the company on the front label. On the back label, it should say "Estate bottled by Cantina Giusto." You might see Cantina Giusto written

on the top of the back label and the words "Estate Bottled" written somewhere else on the back, and that's acceptable.

4. Make sure you see the words "Estate Bottled" on the back label. Don't buy it if it just says "Bottled by…"

5. Avoid wines that that have the word "Coop" or "Cooperativa" on the back label. It's usually found in the sentence where it says "Bottled by Coop…" or "Produced by Cooperativa…"

CHAPTER 39

WHITE WINE $20-$30

5 Checkmarks to Buying Quality Italian White Wine

1. Look for Sicily or Sardegna in your wine shop's Italian section. These are two regions in Italy, and there should be separate signs for each. If not, ask the wine shop manager to show you which wines come from these regions in this price range.

2. Look for Catarratto or Vermentino. These are types of white wine found in Sicily and Sardegna. Catarratto is from Sicily and Vermentino is from Sardegna. The wine type might be found on the front label, the back label, or on both.

3. Make sure the name of the winery, which is printed on the front label, has the same company name on the back. Example: "Cantina Giusto" is the name of the company on the front label. On the back label, it should say "Estate bottled by Cantina Giusto." You might see Cantina Giusto written on the top of the back label and the words "Estate Bottled" written somewhere else on the back, and that's acceptable.

4. Make sure you see the words "Estate Bottled" on the back label. Don't buy it if it says "Bottled by…"

5. Avoid wines that that have the word "Coop" or "Cooperativa" on the back label. It's usually found in the sentence where it says "Bottled by Coop…" or "Produced by Cooperativa…"

CHAPTER 40

RESOURCES

RESOURCES FOR FINDING SMALL ITALIAN PRODUCERS:

Slow Wine - https://www.slowfood.com/what-we-do/themes/slow-wine/

Gladiator Wine Distribution - http://www.gladiatorwine.com/blog

Gladiator Wine Distribution is my importing and distribution company in New York. The wines on my website come from small producers that I personally discovered and vetted during my travels in Italy. These wines are available in New York State and can be shipped to other states. The Gladiator Wine Blog is full of free tips and tricks on pairing food with Italian wines, learning about Italian grape varietals, choosing Italian wines for your special events, and more. If you'd like to buy the small production wines I import, you can click on the following link to see the list of stores that carry them: http://gladiatorwine.com/italian-wine-new-york/

Vinit - http://www.vinit.net

This can be a good reference point for you if you're looking to find out the total bottle production of a winery.

These two other sources are in Italian, but Google Translate should be able to help you out. I enjoy these two sites very much.

Luciano Pignataro Wine Blog - http://www.lucianopignataro.it
Luciano Pignataro comes from the Campania region and is an excellent resource for small producer wineries in Italy. He also shares some amazing pasta recipes that I use all the time.

Cronache di Gusto - http://www.cronachedigusto.it

Cronache di Gusto means "The Taste Chronicles," and it's an excellent source for finding small wineries in Italy. Many of the recommended wineries might not be available in the United States or your country, but some will be. I love reading the reviews and stories about the small artisans.

CHAPTER 41

WHAT IF YOU DON'T HAVE TIME TO FIND A HIDDEN GEM?

I F YOU BELIEVE in the Hidden Gem Formula but you simply don't have the time to go searching for these hidden gems, you can join my wine club called "Hidden Gems of Italy." Once per month, I'll email you a wine recommendation that has met the criteria required to be considered a hidden gem. I'll give you some background information about the grape, the territory, and the producer. I'll even show you where you can buy it so it can be shipped to your home.

To get a free wine recommendation, sign up for free, and I'll send you a "starter wine" right away: http://gladiatorwine.com/hiddengems/

CHAPTER 42

ARRIVEDERCI!

I AM SO excited that you had the curiosity and the passion to learn more about Italian wines. So many people pass by the Italian wine section at their local wine shop, not realizing that they are giving up experiencing the best wines in the world for something easier to understand like a California Merlot.

You are now ready to pursue a lifelong hobby of shopping for hidden gems, understanding how to read Italian wine labels, and most importantly, drinking authentic Italian wines that the Big Wine Industry doesn't want you to know about.

PLEASE KEEP IN TOUCH! FIND ME ON SOCIAL MEDIA:

LinkedIn - https://www.linkedin.com/in/tonymargiotta/

https://www.facebook.com/groups/372712049588169/ - Become a member of my wine community, Italian Wine Enthusiasts of New York. It's a great place to join other like-minded Italian wine lovers, and you can always get in contact with me there.

https://www.facebook.com/GladiatorWine/ - Gladiator Wine's Facebook Page. If you like the wines that my company imports, you can always "like" the page. I also regularly list when I'm doing tastings in New York.

Don't forget to set up an account on the **Delectable App** on your phone. Look me up, Tony Margiotta, and read my random reviews about wines.

Arrivederci! See you soon!

CHAPTER 43

SMALL REQUEST

Thanks again for purchasing my book! It would mean the world to me if you could leave me a review on Amazon. Please turn the page and write your review. I read them all. If you're reading a paperback, please go back to the site you purchased from and write a review.

Good feedback will help me write more books that will help you along your journey in Italian wine. Critical feedback, (but friendly), will help me make improvements when the next edition is released.

Salute, and Cheers!
Tony Margiotta

ABOUT THE AUTHOR

Tony Margiotta is an award-winning wine importer and wine consultant known for his outstanding wine selections—among them Double Gold Medals from the New York International Wine Competition. His company, Gladiator Wine Distribution, specializes in hard-to-find wines from small producers in Italy. To request more information for building an Italian wine collection, wine class, wine event, or to set up a tasting appointment for your business, write to support@gladiatorwine.com.

Made in the
USA
Middletown, DE